STUDY GUIDE / WOR

Essentials of Accounting

Tenth Edition

Michael D. Lawrence, CPA, CMA, CFM
Portland Community College
Portland, Oregon

Joan S. Ryan, MS, MBA, CMA
Clackamas Community College
Oregon City, Oregon

THOMSON
™
SOUTH-WESTERN

Australia · Canada · Mexico · Singapore · Spain · United Kingdom · United States

THOMSON

™

SOUTH-WESTERN

Study Guide / Working Papers
Essentials of Accounting

Michael D. Lawrence ~ Joan S. Ryan

Executive Editors:
Michele Baird, Maureen Staudt, and Michael Stranz

Project Development Manager:
Linda deStefano

Sr. Marketing Coordinators :
Lindsay Annett and Sara Mercurio

Production/Manufacturing Manager:
Donna M. Brown

Production Editorial Manager:
Dan Plofchan

Pre-Media Services Supervisor:
Becki Walker

Rights and Permissions Specialist:
Kalina Ingham Hintz

Cover Image:
Getty Images*

The Adaptable Courseware Program consists of products and additions to existing Thomson products that are produced from camera-ready copy. Peer review, class testing, and accuracy are primarily the responsibility of the author(s).

ISBN 13: 978-0-759-39592-3
ISBN 10: 0-759-39592-6

International Divisions List

Asia (Including India):
Thomson Learning
(a division of Thomson Asia Pte Ltd)
5 Shenton Way #01-01
UIC Building
Singapore 068808
Tel: (65) 6410-1200
Fax: (65) 6410-1208

Australia/New Zealand:
Thomson Learning Australia
102 Dodds Street
Southbank, Victoria 3006
Australia

Latin America:
Thomson Learning
Seneca 53
Colonia Polano
11560 Mexico, D.F., Mexico
Tel (525) 281-2906
Fax (525) 281-2656

Canada:
Thomson Nelson
1120 Birchmount Road
Toronto, Ontario
Canada M1K 5G4
Tel (416) 752-9100
Fax (416) 752-8102

UK/Europe/Middle East/Africa:
Thomson Learning
High Holborn House
50-51 Bedford Row
London, WC1R 4LS
United Kingdom
Tel 44 (020) 7067-2500
Fax 44 (020) 7067-2600

Spain (Includes Portugal):
Thomson Paraninfo
Calle Magallanes 25
28015 Madrid
España
Tel 34 (0)91 446-3350
Fax 34 (0)91 445-6218

CHAPTER 1

THE NATURE OF ACCOUNTING

PRACTICE TEST

Part I—True/False

Please circle the correct answer.

T F 1. The first step in the accounting process is recording.

T F 2. A person who solely records accounting information is referred to as a bookkeeper.

T F 3. The accounting equation can be expressed as A = L + OE.

T F 4. Any activity of a business that affects the accounting equation is called a transaction.

T F 5. The term expense generally means an increase in assets because a sale was made.

T F 6. The balance sheet shows the assets, liabilities, and owner's equity over a period of time.

T F 7. To debit an account means to enter an amount on the left side of the account.

T F 8. A trial balance is a listing of all accounts showing the title and the ending balance.

T F 9. The normal balance of any account will be on the decrease side.

T F 10. A trial balance is a formal statement that will appear with the income statement, statement of owner's equity, and the balance sheet.

Part II—Multiple Choice

Please circle the correct answer.

1. Which of the following is **not** one of the six major phases of the accounting process?
   a. Analyzing
   b. Bookkeeping
   c. Recording
   d. Interpreting

2. The first phase of the accounting process is
   a. Recording
   b. Classifying
   c. Interpreting
   d. Analyzing

3. The final phase of the accounting process is
   a. Summarizing
   b. Reporting
   c. Interpreting
   d. Classifying

4. A common example of an asset is
   a. Accounts payable
   b. Owner's capital
   c. Owner's drawing
   d. Office supplies

Part II—Continued

5.   A common example of a liability is
     a.   Owner's equity
     b.   Office equipment
     c.   Notes payable
     d.   Owner's drawing

6.   The amount by which business assets exceed owner's equity is called
     a.   Liabilities
     b.   Capital
     c.   Cash
     d.   Drawing

7.   The fundamental accounting equation can be expressed as
     a.   Assets = Liabilities – Owner's Equity
     b.   Liabilities = Assets + Owner's Equity
     c.   Assets = Liabilities + Owner's Equity
     d.   Owner's Equity = Liabilities – Assets

8.   An Owner withdrew cash from the business. This transaction affected the accounting equation by
     a.   An increase in a Liability and a decrease in an Asset
     b.   A decrease in an Asset and an increase in a Liability
     c.   A decrease in an Asset and a decrease in Owner's Equity
     d.   An increase and a decrease in Owner's Equity

9.   A business received $3,000 in cash from a client for professional services rendered. This transaction would be entered in the accounting records as
     a.   Debit to Cash and a credit to Accounts Payable
     b.   Debit to Professional Fees and a credit to Cash
     c.   Debit to Owner's Capital and a credit to Cash
     d.   Debit to cash and a credit to Professional Fees

10. A business purchased office supplies for cash, $500. This transaction would be entered in the accounting records as a
     a.   Debit to Cash and a credit to Office Supplies
     b.   Debit to Office Supplies Expense and a credit to Owner's Capital
     c.   Debit to Office Supplies and a credit to Accounts Payable
     d.   Debit to Office Supplies and a credit to Cash

Part III—Fill in the Blank

1.   The difference between assets and liabilities is called _____.

2.   Equities can be divided between _____ and _____.

3.   Transactions are recorded in the accounting records using the _____.

4.   The owner of a business paid a creditor on account. The effect on the accounting equation is to (increase/decrease) _____ a liability account and (increase/decrease) _____ an asset account.

5.   The financial statements must always be prepared in the following order: (1) _____, (2) _____, (3) _____.

6.   The _____ shows the assets, liabilities, and owner's equity of a business as of a specified date.

Part III—Continued

7. To _____ an account means to enter an amount on the left side of the account.

8. To _____ an account means to enter an amount on the right side of the account.

9. A company received $5,000 in cash from a client for professional services rendered. The account titled Cash is (debited/credited) _____ and the account titled Professional Fees is (debited/credited) _____.

10. A _____ is a listing of all accounts showing the title and the ending balance.

Part IV—Practice Problems

Practice Problem 1—Effect of transactions on the Accounting Equation

On January 1, 200X, Phil Jackson, a public accountant, had assets consisting of cash, $15,000; office equipment, $9,000; automobile, $18,300. Accounts payable were $3,000. The following business transactions occurred during the month of January:

(a) Paid office rent for January, $1,200
(b) Paid $1,000 cash for office equipment
(c) Received $3,100 cash for professional services
(d) Paid $320 for telephone service
(e) Paid $2,100 on the account payable
(f) Withdrew $2,000 for personal use

Required:

1. Calculate the beginning balance capital.

2. Enter the balance for each account under the correct column below.

3. Indicate the effect of each transaction on the accounting equation by entering the proper amounts in the columns shown on the following page. Each amount should be preceded by a plus sign if it represents a decrease.

Practice Problem 1—Concluded

	Assets			=	Liabilities	+	Owner's Equity			
	Cash	+ Office Equipment	+ Automobile	=	Accounts Payable	+	P. Jackson Capital	− P. Jackson Drawing	+ Revenue	− Expenses
Bal.	$15,000	+ $9,000	+ $18,300	=	$3,000	+		−	+	−
(a)		+	+							
Bal.		+	+	=		+		−	+	−
(b)		+	+							
Bal.		+	+	=		+		−	+	−
(c)		+	+							
Bal.		+	+	=		+		−	+	−
(d)		+	+							
Bal.		+	+	=		+		−	+	−
(e)		+	+							
Bal.		+	+	=		+		−	+	−
(f)		+	+							
Bal.		+	+	=		+		−	+	−

Practice Problem 2—T Accounts, Trial Balance, and Financial Statements

Andrea Kreitz decided to establish an advertising agency to be known as Columbia Advertising Agency. Kreitz's business transactions for the first month of operations ending July 31, 200X, were as follows:

a.   Kreitz invested $30,000 cash in the business
b.   Paid office rent for one month, $1,400
c.   Purchased office equipment on account, $9,100
d.   Paid cash for office supplies, $725
e.   Paid telephone bill, $175
f.   Received $6,400 for advertising fees earned
g.   Paid $3,700 on account
h.   Received $2,300 for advertising fees earned
i.   Paid $1,600 wages to office secretary
j.   Withdrew $3,000 for personal use

Required:

1.   Using the T accounts below, enter the above transactions. Identify each entry by letter.
2.   Foot the accounts and enter the ending balance on the plus side or larger side.

Cash	Accounts Payable	Advertising Fees

		Rent Expense

Office Supplies	Andrea Kreitz, Capital	Telephone Expense

Office Equipment	Andrea Kreitz, Drawing	Wages Expense

Practice Problem 2—Continued

3. Prepare a trial balance as of July 31, 200X

4. Prepare an income statement for the month ending, July 31, 200X.

Practice Problem 2—Concluded

5. Prepare a Statement of Owner's Equity for the month ending, July 31, 200X

6. Prepare a Balance Sheet as of July 31, 200X.

SOLUTIONS TO PRACTICE TEST

Part I	**Part II**	**Part III**
1. F	1. b	1. owner's equity
2. T	2. d	2. liabilities and owner's equity
3. T	3. c	3. cost principle
4. T	4. d	4. decrease, decrease
5. F	5. c	5. income statement, statement of owner's equity, balance sheet
6. F	6. a	6. balance sheet
7. T	7. c	7. debit
8. T	8. c	8. credit
9. F	9. d	9. debited, credited
10. F	10. d	10. trial balance

Part IV

Practice Problem 1

	Cash	+	Office Equipment	+	Automobile	=	Accounts Payable	+	P. Jackson Capital	−	P. Jackson Drawing	+	Revenue	−	Expenses
Bal.	$15,000	+	$9,000	+	$18,300	=	$3,000	+	$39,300	−		+		−	
(a)	−1,200														+1,200
Bal.	$13,800	+	$9,000	+	$18,300	=	$3,000	+	$39,300	−		+		−	1,200
(b)	−1,000		+1,000												
Bal.	$12,800	+	$10,000	+	$18,300	=	$3,000	+	$39,300	−		+		−	$1,200
(c)	+$3,100												+3,100		
Bal.	$15,900	+	$10,000	+	$18,300	=	$3,000	+	$39,300	−		+	$3,100	−	$1,200
(d)	− 320														+ 320
Bal.	$15,580	+	$10,000	+	$18,300	=	$3,000	+	$39,300	−		+	$3,100	−	$1,520
(e)	−2,100						−2,100								
Bal.	$13,480	+	$10,000	+	$18,300	=	$ 900	+	$39,300	−		+	$3,100	−	$1,520
(f)	−2,000										+2,000				
Bal.	$11,480	+	$10,000	+	$18,300	=	$ 900	+	$39,300	−	$2,000	+	$3,100	−	$1,520

Practice Problem 2

Parts (1) and (2)

Cash		
(a) 30,000	(b) 1,400
(f) 6,400	(d) 725
(h) 2,300	(e) 175
38,700	(g) 3,700
28,100	(i) 1,600
	(j) 3,000
	10,600

Accounts Payable	
(g) 3,700	(c) 9,100
	5,400

Advertising Fees	
	(f) 6,400
	(h) 2,300
	8,700

Rent Expense	
(b) 1,400	

Office Supplies	
(d) 725	

Andrea Kreitz, Capital	
	(a) 30,000

Telephone Expense	
(e) 175	

Office Equipment	
(c) 9,100	

Andrea Kreitz, Drawing	
(j) 3,000	

Wages Expense	
(i) 1,600	

Part 3

Columbia Advertising Agency
Trial Balance
July 31, 200X

	Debit	Credit
Cash	28,100	
Office Supplies	725	
Office Equipment	9,100	
Accounts Payable	5,400	
Andrea Kreitz, Capital	30,000	
Andrea Kreitz, Drawing	3,000	
Advertising Fees	8,700	
Rent Expense	1,400	
Telephone Expense	175	
Wages Expense	1,600	
	44,100	44,100

Part 4

Columbia Advertising Agency
Income Statement
For the Month Ended July 31, 200X

Revenue:		
Advertising Fees		$ 8,700
Expenses:		
Wages Expense	$1,600	
Rent Expense	1,400	
Telephone Expense	175	
Total Expenses	3,175	
Net Income	$ 5,525	

Part 5

Columbia Advertising Agency
Statement of Owner's Equity
For the Month Ended July 31, 200X

Andrea Kreitz, Capital, July 1, 200X	$30,000	
Net income for the month	$ 5,525	
Less withdrawals	3,000	
Net increase in capital		2,525
Andrea Kreitz, Capital, July 31, 200X	$32,525	

Part 6

Columbia Advertising Agency
Balance Sheet
For the Month Ended July 31, 200X

Assets		Liabilities	
Cash	$28,100	Accounts Payable	5,400
Office Supplies	725		
Office Equipment	9,100		
		Owner's Equity	
		Andrea Kreitz, Capital	32,525
		Total Liabilities and	
Total Assets	$37,925	Owner's Equity	$37,925

CHAPTER 1 WORKING PAPERS

EXERCISE 1A-1

1. _____
2. _____
3. _____

EXERCISE 1A-2

	Assets	=	Liabilities	+	Owner's Equity				
	+ −		− +		Capital −	Drawing +	Revenue −	Expenses	
					− +	+ −	− +	+ −	
(a)									
(b)									
(c)									
(d)									
(e)									
(f)									

EXERCISE 1A-3

1.

EXERCISE 1A-3

1.

	Assets			=	Liabilities	+	Owner's Equity						
	Cash	+	Office Equipment	+	Automobile	=	Accounts Payable	+	Capital C. Ball Capital	–	Drawing C. Ball Drawing	+	Revenue	–	Expenses	Description of Expenses
Bal.	$15,000		$8,000		$22,000		$8,200							
(a)													
Bal.													
(b)													
Bal.													
(c)													
Bal.													
(d)													
Bal.													
(e)													
Bal.													
(f)													
Bal.													
Totals													

EXERCISE 1A-3—CONTINUED

2.

EXERCISE 1A-3—CONCLUDED

2.

PROBLEM 1A-4

1.

PROBLEM 1A-4

1.

	Assets			=	Liabilities	+	Owner's Equity					
	Cash	+	Office Equipment	+	Automobile	=	Accounts Payable	+	Capital J. Davis Capital	−	Drawing J. Davis Drawing	+	Revenue	−	Expenses		Description of Expenses
Bal.	$13,500		$9,200		$28,700		$3,900								
(a)															
Bal.															
(b)															
Bal.															
(c)															
Bal.															
(d)															
Bal.															
(e)															
Bal.															
(f)															
Bal.															
(g)															
Bal															
Totals															

PROBLEM 1A-4—CONTINUED

2.

PROBLEM 1A-4—CONCLUDED

2.

PROBLEM 1A-5

1.

PROBLEM 1A-5—CONCLUDED

1.

PROBLEM 1A-6

1.

PROBLEM 1A-6

1.

	Assets			=	Liabilities	+	Owner's Equity						
	Cash	+ Office Equipment	+ Automobile	=	Accounts Payable	+	Capital D. Higgs Capital	– Drawing D. Higgs Drawing	+ Revenue	– Expenses	Description of Expenses
Bal.	$16,350	$14,145	$36,200	=	$3,100						
(a)											
Bal.											
(b)											
Bal.											
(c)											
Bal.											
(d)											
Bal.											
(e)											
Bal.											
(f)											
Bal.											
(g)											
Bal.											
Totals				=							

PROBLEM 1A-6—CONTINUED

2.

PROBLEM 1A-6—CONCLUDED

2.

PROBLEM 1A-7

1.

PROBLEM 1A-7

1.

2.

EXERCISE 1B-8

		Recorded on Debit Side	Recorded on Credit Side
a.	Increase in cash account	_____	_____
b.	Decrease in accounts payable account	_____	_____
c.	Increase in owner's capital account	_____	_____
d.	Increase in owner's drawing account	_____	_____
e.	Increase in expense account	_____	_____
f.	Increase in revenue account	_____	_____
g.	Increase in accounts payable account	_____	_____

EXERCISE 1B-9

Assets	=	Liabilities	+	Owner's Equity	+	Revenue	−	Expense

EXERCISE 1B-10

_____

_____

ACCOUNT	DEBIT	CREDIT

PROBLEM 1B-11

1.—3.

Cash	Office Supplies	Office Equipment

Accounts Payable	Debbie Summer, Capital	Debbie Summer, Drawing

Advertising Fees	Rent Expense	Telephone Expense

Wages Expense

PROBLEM 1B-11—CONCLUDED

4.

ACCOUNT	DEBIT	CREDIT

PROBLEM 1B-12

ACCOUNT	DEBIT	CREDIT

PROBLEM 1B-13

1.—3.

Cash	Office Supplies	Office Equipment

Accounts Payable	Michael Eary, Capital	Michael Eary, Drawing

Advertising Fees	Rent Expense	Telephone Expense

Wages Expense

PROBLEM 1B-13—CONCLUDED

4.

ACCOUNT	DEBIT	CREDIT

PROBLEM 1B-14

ACCOUNT	DEBIT	CREDIT

CHALLENGE PROBLEM
1.—3.

Cash	Office Supplies	Office Equipment

Accounts Payable	Denise Snyder, Capital	Denise Snyder, Drawing

Professional Fees	Rent Expense	Telephone Expense

Advertising Expense	Wages Expense

CHALLENGE PROBLEM—CONTINUED
4.

Mind Research Institute		
Trial Balance		
September 30, 200X		
ACCOUNT	DEBIT	CREDIT

CHALLENGE PROBLEM—CONTINUED
5.

Mind Research Institute

Income Statement

For the Month Ended September 30, 200X

CHALLENGE PROBLEM—CONTINUED

6.

Mind Research Institute

Statement of Owner's Equity

For the Month Ended September 30, 200X

7.

Mind Research Institute

Balance Sheet

September 30, 200X

CHAPTER 2

ACCOUNTING PROCEDURE

PRACTICE TEST

Part I—True/False

Please circle the correct answer.

T F 1. A source document contains data that affects a business and should be entered into its books.

T F 2. The accounting cycle begins with journalizing transactions into the general journal.

T F 3. Bill Adams, Drawing, is an example of a temporary account.

T F 4. You would typically find a revenue account numbered as a 300 account.

T F 5. The posting reference column is used to record credit entries in a general journal.

T F 6. All amounts in the general journal are posted to general ledger accounts so that balances may be kept during the month.

T F 7. The trial balance is a listing of all accounts and their balances at the end of the accounting period.

T F 8. When journalizing transactions, the account being debited is entered before the account being credited.

T F 9. The balance sheet shows the results of the operation of the business during the month, while the income statement shows the status of the business.

T F 10. The statement of owner's equity reports revenue and expenses for the period.

Part II—Multiple Choice

Please circle the correct answer.

1. Which of these financial statements is always prepared first?
    a. The trial balance
    b. The income statement
    c. The statement of owner's equity
    d. The balance sheet

2. When expenses are compared to revenues for the period, the financial statement that summarizes this is the:
    a. Income Statement
    b. Statement of Owner's Equity
    c. Balance Sheet
    d. Trial Balance

3. Which of these is a source document?
    a. The general ledger
    b. The general journal
    c. A receipt
    d. A journal entry

4. Which of these is a temporary account?
    a. Cash
    b. Accounts Receivable
    c. Rent Expense
    d. B. Jones, Capital

Part II—Continued

5.   Which of these is a permanent account?
        a.   B. Jones, Drawing
        b.   Professional Fees
        c.   Telephone Expense
        d.   Office Equipment

6.   The accounting cycle begins with which one of these?
        a.   Journalizing transactions
        b.   Posting transactions
        c.   The trial balance
        d.   Analyzing source documents

7.   Within a chart of accounts, the number 221 would likely refer to a(n) _____ account.
        a.   Asset
        b.   Liability
        c.   Owner's equity
        d.   Revenue

8.   Within a chart of accounts, the number 511 would likely refer to a(n) _____ account.
        a.   Expense
        b.   Asset
        c.   Liability
        d.   Revenue

9.   Which of these accounts would appear on the income statement?
        a.   Accounts Payable
        b.   Rent Expense
        c.   G. Smith, Drawing
        d.   G. Smith, Capital

10.   Which of these accounts would appear on the balance sheet?
        a.   Rent Expense
        b.   Professional Fees
        c.   Office Equipment
        d.   M. Black, Drawing

Part III—Fill in the Blank

1.   Each transaction begins with a _____ which is a piece of paper containing data that affects a business.

2.   After journalizing, transactions are _____ to the general ledger accounts.

3.   Cash, accounts payable, and the capital account are all examples of _____ accounts.

4.   When revenues exceed expenses at the end of the period, it is called _____.

5.   The _____ form of balance sheet is arranged with assets on the left side and liabilities and owner's equity on the right side.

6.   The _____ is a book of original entry because it is where the first accounting record of a transaction is made.

7.   When payment is made on account to an existing creditor, _____ is the account that is debited.

Part III—Continued

8.   When general journal page numbers are posted from the general journal to the general ledger account, the process is called _____ because you can trace where entries came from.

9.   When the trial balance proves that debits equal credits, this (is, is not) proof that there are no errors in journalizing or posting.

10.   The statement of owner's equity reports beginning capital plus _____, minus withdrawals by the owner during the period.

Part IV—Practice Problems

Problem 1—Journal Entries

Required:

1.   Using a general journal, prepare journal entries for the following transactions of R. Adams.

   a.   The owner invests $10,000 cash in the business.
   b.   The owner purchases $5,000 worth of equipment on account.
   c.   The owner pays the rent, $500.
   d.   Cash of $2,500 is received for services rendered.
   e.   The owner withdraws $500 in cash.
   f.   A payment of $250 is made on equipment previously purchased on account.
   g.   Services worth $1,000 are rendered; payment will be due next month.
   h. $500 is received on account for services rendered in (g) above.

Practice Problem 1—Concluded

GENERAL JOURNAL

PAGE 4

	DATE		DESCRIPTION	POST REF.	DEBIT	CREDIT	
1							1
2							2
3							3
4							4
5							5
6							6
7							7
8							8
9							9
10							10
11							11
12							12
13							13
14							14
15							15
16							16
17							17
18							18
19							19
20							20
21							21
22							22
23							23
24							24
25							25
26							26
27							27
28							28
29							29
30							30
31							31
32							32
33							33
34							34
35							35

Problem 2—Financial Statements

Required:

Prepare the financial statements for Jack's Shoe Repair for the month ended December 31, 200X, based on the following information:

Jack's Shoe Repair
Trial Balance
December 31, 200X

	Debit	Credit
Cash	3,500	
Accounts Receivable	5,800	
Equipment	11,000	
Accounts Payable		3,000
Notes Payable		4,000
Jack Mills, Capital		13,500
Jack Mills, Drawing	2,000	
Repair Revenue	3,000	
Rent Expense	1,000	
Telephone Expense	200	
	23,500	23,500

Practice Problem—Continued

Income Statement

Statement of Owner's Equity

Practice Problem—Concluded

Balance Sheet

SOLUTIONS TO PRACTICE TEST

Part I	Part II	Part III
1. T	1. b	1. source document
2. F	2. a	2. posted
3. T	3. c	3. permanent
4. F	4. c	4. net income
5. F	5. d	5. account
6. T	6. d	6. general journal
7. T	7. b	7. accounts payable
8. T	8. a	8. cross reference
9. F	9. b	9. is not
10. F	10. c	10. net income

Part IV

PROBLEM 1

GENERAL JOURNAL

PAGE 4

DATE	DESCRIPTION	POST REF.	DEBIT	CREDIT
a.	Cash		10,000	
	R. Adams, Capital			10,000
	Investment			
b.	Equipment		5,000	
	Accounts Payable			5,000
	Purchase equipment on account			
c.	Rent Expense		500	
	Cash			500
	Paid the rent			
d.	Cash		2,500	
	Service Revenue			2,500
	Services performed for cash			
e.	R. Adams, Drawing		500	
	Cash			500
	Owner's withdrawal			
f.	Accounts Payable		250	
	Cash			250
	Payment on account			
g.	Accounts Receivable		1,000	
	Service Revenue			1,000
	Services performed on account			
h.	Cash		500	
	Accounts Receivable			500
	Received on account			

Practice Problem 2

Jack's Shoe Repair
Income Statement
For the Month Ended December 31, 200X

Revenue:		
Repair fees		$3,000
Expenses:		
Rent expense	$1,000	
Telephone expense	200	
Total expenses		1,200
Net income		$1,800

Jack's Shoe Repair
Statement of Owner's Equity
For the Month Ended December 31, 200X

Jack Mills, capital, December 1, 200X		$13,500
Withdrawals by owner	$2,000	
Net income	1,800	
Net decrease in capital		200
Jack Mills, capital, December 31, 200X		$13,300

Jack's Shoe Repair
Balance Sheet
December 31, 200X

Assets:		
Cash		$ 3,500
Accounts receivable		5,800
Equipment		11,000
Total assets		$20,300
Liabilities:		
Accounts payable	$3,000	
Notes payable	4,000	
Total liabilities		$ 7,000
Owner's Equity:		
Jack Mills, capital		$13,300
Total liabilities and owner's equity		$20,300

CHAPTER 2 WORKING PAPERS
EXERCISE 2A-1

Lin Appliance Repair Company
Chart of Accounts

Assets:

———— Cash
———— Accounts Receivable
———— Office Supplies
———— Equipment

Liabilities:

———— Accounts Payable
———— Notes Payable

Owner's Equity:

———— Jui-Fen Lin, Capital
———— Jui-Fen Lin, Drawing

Revenue:

———— Repair Fees

Expenses:

———— Salary Expense
———— Rent Expense
———— Telephone Expense
———— Travel Expense
———— Advertising Expense
———— Utilities Expense
———— Miscellaneous Expense

EXERCISE 2A-2

GENERAL JOURNAL   PAGE 4

	DATE	DESCRIPTION	POST REF.	DEBIT	CREDIT	
1						1
2						2
3						3
4						4
5						5
6						6
7						7
8						8
9						9
10						10
11						11
12						12
13						13
14						14
15						15
16						16
17						17
18						18
19						19
20						20
21						21
22						22

EXERCISE 2A-2—CONCLUDED

GENERAL JOURNAL

	DATE	DESCRIPTION	POST REF.	DEBIT	CREDIT	
1						1
2						2
3						3
4						4
5						5
6						6
7						7
8						8
9						9
10						10
11						11
12						12
13						13
14						14
15						15
16						16
17						17
18						18
19						19
20						20
21						21
22						22
23						23
24						24
25						25
26						26
27						27
28						28
29						29
30						30
31						31
32						32
33						33
34						34
35						35
36						36

EXERCISE 2A-3

General Ledger

ACCOUNT Cash   ACCOUNT NO. 111

DATE	ITEM	POST REF.	DEBIT	CREDIT	BALANCE	
					DEBIT	CREDIT

ACCOUNT Office Supplies   ACCOUNT NO. 121

DATE	ITEM	POST REF.	DEBIT	CREDIT	BALANCE	
					DEBIT	CREDIT

ACCOUNT Accounts Payable   ACCOUNT NO. 211

DATE	ITEM	POST REF.	DEBIT	CREDIT	BALANCE	
					DEBIT	CREDIT

ACCOUNT Notes Payable   ACCOUNT NO. 221

DATE	ITEM	POST REF.	DEBIT	CREDIT	BALANCE	
					DEBIT	CREDIT

EXERCISE 2A-3—CONCLUDED

ACCOUNT A. Salazar, Capital   ACCOUNT NO. 311

DATE	ITEM	POST REF.	DEBIT	CREDIT	BALANCE	
					DEBIT	CREDIT

ACCOUNT A. Salazar, Drawing   ACCOUNT NO. 312

DATE	ITEM	POST REF.	DEBIT	CREDIT	BALANCE	
					DEBIT	CREDIT

ACCOUNT Service Revenue   ACCOUNT NO. 411

DATE	ITEM	POST REF.	DEBIT	CREDIT	BALANCE	
					DEBIT	CREDIT

ACCOUNT Rent Expense   ACCOUNT NO. 511

DATE	ITEM	POST REF.	DEBIT	CREDIT	BALANCE	
					DEBIT	CREDIT

ACCOUNT Telephone Expense   ACCOUNT NO. 521

DATE	ITEM	POST REF.	DEBIT	CREDIT	BALANCE	
					DEBIT	CREDIT

PROBLEM 2A-4

PROBLEM 2A-5

1.   **GENERAL JOURNAL**   PAGE 1

	DATE	DESCRIPTION	POST REF.	DEBIT	CREDIT	
1						1
2						2
3						3
4						4
5						5
6						6
7						7
8						8
9						9
10						10
11						11
12						12
13						13
14						14
15						15
16						16
17						17
18						18
19						19
20						20
21						21
22						22
23						23
24						24
25						25
26						26
27						27
28						28
29						29
30						30
31						31
32						32
33						33
34						34
35						35
36						36

PROBLEM 2A-5—CONTINUED

1.   **GENERAL JOURNAL**   PAGE 2

	DATE		DESCRIPTION	POST REF.	DEBIT	CREDIT	
1							1
2							2
3							3
4							4
5							5
6							6
7							7
8							8
9							9
10							10
11							11
12							12
13							13
14							14
15							15
16							16
17							17
18							18
19							19
20							20
21							21
22							22
23							23
24							24
25							25
26							26
27							27
28							28
29							29
30							30
31							31
32							32
33							33
34							34
35							35
36							36

PROBLEM 2A-5—CONTINUED

General Ledger

2.

ACCOUNT Cash   ACCOUNT NO. 111

DATE	ITEM	POST REF.	DEBIT	CREDIT	BALANCE DEBIT	BALANCE CREDIT

ACCOUNT Accounts Receivable   ACCOUNT NO. 121

DATE	ITEM	POST REF.	DEBIT	CREDIT	BALANCE DEBIT	BALANCE CREDIT

ACCOUNT Cleaning Equipment   ACCOUNT NO. 131

DATE	ITEM	POST REF.	DEBIT	CREDIT	BALANCE DEBIT	BALANCE CREDIT

ACCOUNT Accounts Payable   ACCOUNT NO. 211

DATE	ITEM	POST REF.	DEBIT	CREDIT	BALANCE DEBIT	BALANCE CREDIT

PROBLEM 2A-5—CONTINUED

2.

ACCOUNT Notes Payable    ACCOUNT NO. 221

DATE	ITEM	POST REF.	DEBIT	CREDIT	BALANCE DEBIT	BALANCE CREDIT

ACCOUNT James Miller, Capital   ACCOUNT NO. 311

DATE	ITEM	POST REF.	DEBIT	CREDIT	BALANCE DEBIT	BALANCE CREDIT

ACCOUNT James Miller, Drawing   ACCOUNT NO. 312

DATE	ITEM	POST REF.	DEBIT	CREDIT	BALANCE DEBIT	BALANCE CREDIT

ACCOUNT Service Revenue   ACCOUNT NO. 411

DATE	ITEM	POST REF.	DEBIT	CREDIT	BALANCE DEBIT	BALANCE CREDIT

PROBLEM 2A-5—CONCLUDED

2.

ACCOUNT Rent Expense   ACCOUNT NO. 511

DATE	ITEM	POST REF.	DEBIT	CREDIT	BALANCE	
					DEBIT	CREDIT

ACCOUNT Telephone Expense   ACCOUNT NO. 521

DATE	ITEM	POST REF.	DEBIT	CREDIT	BALANCE	
					DEBIT	CREDIT

ACCOUNT Utility Expense   ACCOUNT NO. 531

DATE	ITEM	POST REF.	DEBIT	CREDIT	BALANCE	
					DEBIT	CREDIT

ACCOUNT Miscellaneous Expense   ACCOUNT NO. 599

DATE	ITEM	POST REF.	DEBIT	CREDIT	BALANCE	
					DEBIT	CREDIT

PROBLEM 2A-6

PROBLEM 2A-7

1.   **GENERAL JOURNAL**   PAGE 1

	DATE		DESCRIPTION	POST REF.	DEBIT	CREDIT	
1							1
2							2
3							3
4							4
5							5
6							6
7							7
8							8
9							9
10							10
11							11
12							12
13							13
14							14
15							15
16							16
17							17
18							18
19							19
20							20
21							21
22							22
23							23
24							24
25							25
26							26
27							27
28							28
29							29
30							30
31							31
32							32
33							33
34							34
35							35
36							36

PROBLEM 2A-7—CONTINUED

1.   **GENERAL JOURNAL**   PAGE 2

	DATE		DESCRIPTION	POST REF.	DEBIT	CREDIT	
1							1
2							2
3							3
4							4
5							5
6							6
7							7
8							8
9							9
10							10
11							11
12							12
13							13
14							14
15							15
16							16
17							17
18							18
19							19
20							20
21							21
22							22
23							23
24							24
25							25
26							26
27							27
28							28
29							29
30							30
31							31
32							32
33							33
34							34
35							35
36							36

PROBLEM 2A-7—CONTINUED

2.

General Ledger

ACCOUNT Cash   ACCOUNT NO. 111

DATE	ITEM	POST REF.	DEBIT	CREDIT	BALANCE DEBIT	BALANCE CREDIT

ACCOUNT Accounts Receivable   ACCOUNT NO. 121

DATE	ITEM	POST REF.	DEBIT	CREDIT	BALANCE DEBIT	BALANCE CREDIT

ACCOUNT Office Equipment   ACCOUNT NO. 141

DATE	ITEM	POST REF.	DEBIT	CREDIT	BALANCE DEBIT	BALANCE CREDIT

ACCOUNT Accounts Payable   ACCOUNT NO. 211

DATE	ITEM	POST REF.	DEBIT	CREDIT	BALANCE DEBIT	BALANCE CREDIT

PROBLEM 2A-7—CONTINUED

2.

ACCOUNT Notes Payable   ACCOUNT NO. 221

DATE	ITEM	POST REF.	DEBIT	CREDIT	BALANCE	
					DEBIT	CREDIT

ACCOUNT Ryan Phan, Capital   ACCOUNT NO. 311

DATE	ITEM	POST REF.	DEBIT	CREDIT	BALANCE	
					DEBIT	CREDIT

ACCOUNT Ryan Phan, Drawing   ACCOUNT NO. 312

DATE	ITEM	POST REF.	DEBIT	CREDIT	BALANCE	
					DEBIT	CREDIT

ACCOUNT Landscaping Fees   ACCOUNT NO. 411

DATE	ITEM	POST REF.	DEBIT	CREDIT	BALANCE	
					DEBIT	CREDIT

ACCOUNT Rent Expense   ACCOUNT NO. 511

DATE	ITEM	POST REF.	DEBIT	CREDIT	BALANCE	
					DEBIT	CREDIT

PROBLEM 2A-7—CONCLUDED

2.

ACCOUNT Telephone Expense   ACCOUNT NO. 521

DATE	ITEM	POST REF.	DEBIT	CREDIT	BALANCE DEBIT	BALANCE CREDIT

ACCOUNT Utility Expense   ACCOUNT NO. 531

DATE	ITEM	POST REF.	DEBIT	CREDIT	BALANCE DEBIT	BALANCE CREDIT

ACCOUNT Miscellaneous Expense   ACCOUNT NO. 599

DATE	ITEM	POST REF.	DEBIT	CREDIT	BALANCE DEBIT	BALANCE CREDIT

EXERCISE 2B-8

Trial Balance

EXERCISE 2B-9

	Income Statement										

PROBLEM 2B-10

	Income Statement										

PROBLEM 2B-11

Statement of Owner's Equity

PROBLEM 2B-12

Balance Sheet

PROBLEM 2B-13

1.

	Trial Balance

2.

	Income Statement

PROBLEM 2B-14

Statement of Owner's Equity									

PROBLEM 2B-15

Balance Sheet									

CHALLENGE PROBLEM

1.   **GENERAL JOURNAL**   PAGE 8

	DATE		DESCRIPTION	POST REF.	DEBIT	CREDIT	
1							1
2							2
3							3
4							4
5							5
6							6
7							7
8							8
9							9
10							10
11							11
12							12
13							13
14							14
15							15
16							16
17							17
18							18
19							19
20							20
21							21
22							22
23							23
24							24
25							25
26							26
27							27
28							28
29							29
30							30
31							31
32							32
33							33
34							34
35							35
36							36

CHALLENGE PROBLEM—CONTINUED

1. GENERAL JOURNAL PAGE 9

	DATE		DESCRIPTION	POST REF.	DEBIT	CREDIT	
1							1
2							2
3							3
4							4
5							5
6							6
7							7
8							8
9							9
10							10
11							11
12							12
13							13
14							14
15							15
16							16
17							17
18							18
19							19
20							20
21							21
22							22
23							23
24							24
25							25
26							26
27							27
28							28
29							29
30							30
31							31
32							32
33							33
34							34
35							35
36							36

CHALLENGE PROBLEM—CONTINUED

General Ledger

2.

ACCOUNT Cash   ACCOUNT NO. 111

DATE	ITEM	POST REF.	DEBIT	CREDIT	BALANCE	
					DEBIT	CREDIT

ACCOUNT Accounts Receivable   ACCOUNT NO. 121

DATE	ITEM	POST REF.	DEBIT	CREDIT	BALANCE	
					DEBIT	CREDIT

ACCOUNT Office Supplies   ACCOUNT NO. 131

DATE	ITEM	POST REF.	DEBIT	CREDIT	BALANCE	
					DEBIT	CREDIT

CHALLENGE PROBLEM—CONTINUED

2.

ACCOUNT Office Equipment   ACCOUNT NO. 141

DATE	ITEM	POST REF.	DEBIT	CREDIT	BALANCE	
					DEBIT	CREDIT

ACCOUNT Accounts Payable   ACCOUNT NO. 211

DATE	ITEM	POST REF.	DEBIT	CREDIT	BALANCE	
					DEBIT	CREDIT

ACCOUNT Matt Hunt, Capital   ACCOUNT NO. 311

DATE	ITEM	POST REF.	DEBIT	CREDIT	BALANCE	
					DEBIT	CREDIT

ACCOUNT Matt Hunt, Drawing   ACCOUNT NO. 312

DATE	ITEM	POST REF.	DEBIT	CREDIT	BALANCE	
					DEBIT	CREDIT

CHALLENGE PROBLEM—CONTINUED

2.

ACCOUNT Research Fees   ACCOUNT NO. 411

DATE	ITEM	POST REF.	DEBIT	CREDIT	BALANCE DEBIT	BALANCE CREDIT

ACCOUNT Rent Expense   ACCOUNT NO. 511

DATE	ITEM	POST REF.	DEBIT	CREDIT	BALANCE DEBIT	BALANCE CREDIT

ACCOUNT Utilities Expense   ACCOUNT NO. 522

DATE	ITEM	POST REF.	DEBIT	CREDIT	BALANCE DEBIT	BALANCE CREDIT

ACCOUNT Telephone Expense   ACCOUNT NO. 533

DATE	ITEM	POST REF.	DEBIT	CREDIT	BALANCE DEBIT	BALANCE CREDIT

CHALLENGE PROBLEM—CONTINUED

2.

ACCOUNT   CHARITABLE CONTRIBUTIONS EXPENSE   ACCOUNT NO. 543

DATE	ITEM	POST REF.	DEBIT	CREDIT	BALANCE	
					DEBIT	CREDIT

ACCOUNT   Salary Expense   ACCOUNT NO. 555

DATE	ITEM	POST REF.	DEBIT	CREDIT	BALANCE	
					DEBIT	CREDIT

ACCOUNT   TRAVEL AND ENTERTAINMENT EXPENSE   ACCOUNT NO. 577

DATE	ITEM	POST REF.	DEBIT	CREDIT	BALANCE	
					DEBIT	CREDIT

ACCOUNT   Miscellaneous Expense   ACCOUNT NO. 599

DATE	ITEM	POST REF.	DEBIT	CREDIT	BALANCE	
					DEBIT	CREDIT

CHALLENGE PROBLEM—CONTINUED
3.

Trial Balance

CHALLENGE PROBLEM—CONTINUED
4.

Income Statement			

CHALLENGE PROBLEM—CONCLUDED

5.

Statement of Owner's Equity

6.

Balance Sheet

COMPREHENSIVE REVIEW PROBLEM 1

Williams Delivery Services
Chart of Accounts

Assets:

Cash	111
Accounts Receivable	121
Office Supplies	131
Office Equipment	141
Delivery Truck	151

Liabilities:

Accounts Payable	211
Notes Payable	221

Owner's Equity:

Bert Williams, Capital	311
Bert Williams, Drawing	312

Revenue:

Delivery Fees	411

Expenses:

Rent Expense	511
Telephone Expense	521
Charitable Contributions Expense	531
Salary Expense	541
Truck Repair Expense	551
Advertising Expense	561
Utilities Expense	571

COMPREHENSIVE REVIEW PROBLEM 1

1.

GENERAL JOURNAL

	DATE		DESCRIPTION	POST REF.	DEBIT	CREDIT	
1							1
2							2
3							3
4							4
5							5
6							6
7							7
8							8
9							9
10							10
11							11
12							12
13							13
14							14
15							15
16							16
17							17
18							18
19							19
20							20
21							21
22							22
23							23
24							24
25							25
26							26
27							27
28							28
29							29
30							30
31							31
32							32
33							33
34							34
35							35
36							36

COMPREHENSIVE REVIEW PROBLEM 1—CONTINUED

1.

GENERAL JOURNAL

PAGE 2

	DATE		DESCRIPTION	POST REF.	DEBIT	CREDIT	
1							1
2							2
3							3
4							4
5							5
6							6
7							7
8							8
9							9
10							10
11							11
12							12
13							13
14							14
15							15
16							16
17							17
18							18
19							19
20							20
21							21
22							22
23							23
24							24
25							25
26							26
27							27
28							28
29							29
30							30
31							31
32							32
33							33
34							34
35							35
36							36

COMPREHENSIVE REVIEW PROBLEM 1—CONTINUED

2.

ACCOUNT   Cash   ACCOUNT NO. 111

DATE	ITEM	POST REF.	DEBIT	CREDIT	BALANCE	
					DEBIT	CREDIT

ACCOUNT   Accounts Receivable   ACCOUNT NO. 121

DATE	ITEM	POST REF.	DEBIT	CREDIT	BALANCE	
					DEBIT	CREDIT

ACCOUNT   Office Supplies   ACCOUNT NO. 131

DATE	ITEM	POST REF.	DEBIT	CREDIT	BALANCE	
					DEBIT	CREDIT

COMPREHENSIVE REVIEW PROBLEM 1—CONTINUED

2.

ACCOUNT   Office Equipment   ACCOUNT NO. 141

DATE	ITEM	POST REF.	DEBIT	CREDIT	BALANCE	
					DEBIT	CREDIT

ACCOUNT   Delivery Truck   ACCOUNT NO. 151

DATE	ITEM	POST REF.	DEBIT	CREDIT	BALANCE	
					DEBIT	CREDIT

ACCOUNT   Accounts Payable   ACCOUNT NO. 211

DATE	ITEM	POST REF.	DEBIT	CREDIT	BALANCE	
					DEBIT	CREDIT

ACCOUNT   Notes Payable   ACCOUNT NO. 221

DATE	ITEM	POST REF.	DEBIT	CREDIT	BALANCE	
					DEBIT	CREDIT

COMPREHENSIVE REVIEW PROBLEM 1—CONTINUED

2.

ACCOUNT   Bert Williams, Capital   ACCOUNT NO. 311

DATE	ITEM	POST REF.	DEBIT	CREDIT	BALANCE	
					DEBIT	CREDIT

ACCOUNT   Bert Williams, Drawing   ACCOUNT NO. 312

DATE	ITEM	POST REF.	DEBIT	CREDIT	BALANCE	
					DEBIT	CREDIT

ACCOUNT   Delivery Fees   ACCOUNT NO. 411

DATE	ITEM	POST REF.	DEBIT	CREDIT	BALANCE	
					DEBIT	CREDIT

ACCOUNT   Rent Expense   ACCOUNT NO. 511

DATE	ITEM	POST REF.	DEBIT	CREDIT	BALANCE	
					DEBIT	CREDIT

ACCOUNT   Telephone Expense   ACCOUNT NO. 521

DATE	ITEM	POST REF.	DEBIT	CREDIT	BALANCE	
					DEBIT	CREDIT

COMPREHENSIVE REVIEW PROBLEM 1—CONTINUED

2.

ACCOUNT   Charitable Contributions Expense   ACCOUNT NO. 531

DATE	ITEM	POST REF.	DEBIT	CREDIT	BALANCE	
					DEBIT	CREDIT

ACCOUNT   Salary Expense   ACCOUNT NO. 541

DATE	ITEM	POST REF.	DEBIT	CREDIT	BALANCE	
					DEBIT	CREDIT

ACCOUNT   Truck Repair Expense   ACCOUNT NO. 551

DATE	ITEM	POST REF.	DEBIT	CREDIT	BALANCE	
					DEBIT	CREDIT

ACCOUNT   Advertising Expense   ACCOUNT NO. 561

DATE	ITEM	POST REF.	DEBIT	CREDIT	BALANCE	
					DEBIT	CREDIT

ACCOUNT   Utilities Expense   ACCOUNT NO. 571

DATE	ITEM	POST REF.	DEBIT	CREDIT	BALANCE	
					DEBIT	CREDIT

COMPREHENSIVE REVIEW PROBLEM 1—CONTINUED

3.

Trial Balance

COMPREHENSIVE REVIEW PROBLEM 1—CONTINUED

4.

Income Statement

5.

Statement of Owner's Equity

COMPREHENSIVE REVIEW PROBLEM 1—CONCLUDED

6.

Balance Sheet

CHAPTER 3

THE END-OF-PERIOD WORK SHEET

PRACTICE TEST

Part I—True/False

Please circle the correct answer.

T F 1. The accounting cycle is the term used to describe the steps involved in accounting for all of the business activities during a time period.

T F 2. A work sheet is a formal statement that is included with the income statement, statement of owner's equity, and balance sheet.

T F 3. Adjusting entries are needed in order to bring certain accounts up to date.

T F 4. The matching principle states that every transaction must have an equal debit and credit.

T F 5. All adjusting entries will affect one balance sheet account title and one income statement account title.

T F 6. A contra-asset is an offsetting or opposite account and should be deducted from the related asset account.

T F 7. The current market value of an asset is referred to as book value.

T F 8. If total debits exceed total credits in the income statement columns of the work sheet, the difference represents a net income.

T F 9. The statement of owner's equity is considered the connecting link between the income statement and the balance sheet.

T F 10. A formal statement of the assets, liabilities, and owner's equity as of a specific date is an income statement.

Part II—Multiple Choice

Please circle the correct answer.

1. The first step of the accounting cycle is
    a. Journalizing transactions in the general journal
    b. Analyzing source documents
    c. Posting transactions from the general journal to the general ledger
    d. Preparing a trial balance

2. The first pair of amount columns in the work sheet are the
    a. Adjustments columns
    b. Adjusted trial balance columns
    c. Income statement columns
    d. Trial balance columns

3. The matching principle relates to the matching of
    a. Debits and credits
    b. Income statement and balance sheet
    c. Revenues and expenses
    d. General journal and general ledger

4. The unadjusted balance of Supplies is $965. The ending inventory of Supplies is $195. The amount of Supplies Expense for the period is
    a. $195
    b. $965
    c. $1,160
    d. $770

Part II—Continued

5. The unadjusted balance of prepaid insurance is $2,800. The amount of expired insurance is $1,200. The amount of insurance expense for the period is
    a. $1,600
    b. $1,200
    c. $2,800
    d. $4,000

6. An automobile costs $18,000 and has an estimated salvage value of $4,000 at the end of 4 years. The annual amount of depreciation is
    a. $4,000
    b. $4,500
    c. $3,500
    d. $5,500

7. Salaries of $2,500 are paid every Friday for a five day work week. If the end of the year falls on Wednesday, the amount of the adjusting entry is
    a. $2,500
    b. $500
    c. $2,000
    d. $1,500

8. The unadjusted balance of supplies is $680. The ending inventory of supplies is $200. The correct adjusting entry is to
    a. Debit Supplies Expense and credit Supplies for $200
    b. Debit Supplies Expense and credit Supplies for $480
    c. Debit Supplies Expense and credit Supplies for $880
    d. Debit Supplies and credit Supplies Expense for $200

9. The unadjusted balance of prepaid insurance is $4,300. The amount of insurance expired is $2,400. The correct adjusting entry is to
    a. Debit Insurance Expense and credit Prepaid Insurance for $1,900
    b. Debit Insurance Expense and credit Prepaid Insurance for $7,700
    c. Debit Insurance Expense and credit Prepaid Insurance for $2,400
    d. Debit Prepaid Insurance and credit Insurance Expense for $1,900

10. The income statement debit column on the work sheet shows a total of $54,800. The income statement credit column on the work sheet shows a total of $65,000. This would indicate that
    a. There is a net income of $10,200
    b. There is a net loss of $10,200
    c. A net income or net loss cannot be determined until the difference in the balance sheet debit and credit column of the work sheet is calculated
    d. There is a net income of $65,000

Part III—Fill in the Blank

1. The _____ is the term used to describe the steps involved in the accounting for all of the business activities during a time period.

2. Financial statements covering less than a year are called _____.

3. A _____ is used by accountants at the end of the accounting period to make the last steps of the accounting cycle easier.

4. At the end of an accounting period, _____ are needed in order to bring certain accounts up to date.

Part III—Concluded

5. The _____ states that the amount of revenue earned during an accounting period must be matched with the expenses incurred to generate that revenue.

6. All adjusting entries will affect one _____, account title and one _____, account title.

7. The term _____ refers to the process of allocating the cost of a depreciable asset over its useful life.

8. A _____ is an asset like office equipment or an automobile that will last for more than a year.

9. A _____ is an offsetting or opposite account and should be deducted from the related asset account.

10. The difference between the asset account and its related accumulated depreciation is known as the _____.

Part IV—Practice Problems

Problem 1—Analyzing Adjusting Entries and Completing a Work Sheet

Jessie Simpson started a business called Simpson's Music Training. After the first month of operations, the trial balance as of January 31 appears as follows:

Simpson's Music Training
Work Sheet (Partial)
For the Month Ended January 31, 2000X

| | Trial Balance | | Adjustments | |
Account Title	Debit	Credit	Debit	Credit
Cash	1,800.00			
Music Supplies	930.00			
Prepaid Insurance	860.00			
Musical Instruments	9,300.00			
Accum. Depr.—Music Instr.				
Accounts Payable		940.00		
Salaries Payable				
J. Simpson, Capital		6,590.00		
J. Simpson, Drawing	2,000.00			
Income from Services		9,575.00		
Rent Expense	975.00			
Depr. Expense—Music Instr.				
Salary Expense	850.00			
Utilities Expense	330.00			
Music Supplies Expense				
Insurance Expense				
Miscellaneous Expense	60.00			
	17,105.00	17,105.00		

Required:

1. Analyze the following adjustments and enter them on the work sheet on the next two facing pages
   - (a) Ending music supplies inventory as of January 31, $210.
   - (b) Insurance Expired, $770
   - (c) Depreciation of music equipment, $900
   - (d) Salaries earned but not paid as of January 31, $125
2. Complete the work sheet.

Practice Problem 1—Continued

Simpson's Music Training

Work Sheet

For the Month Ended January 31, 200X

	ACCOUNT TITLE	TRIAL BALANCE DEBIT					TRIAL BALANCE CREDIT					ADJUSTMENTS DEBIT					ADJUSTMENTS CREDIT				
1	Cash	1	8	0	0	00															
2	Music Supplies		9	3	0	00															
3	Prepaid Insurance		8	6	0	00															
4	Musical Instruments	9	3	0	0	00															
5	Accum. Depr.—Music Instruments	9	3	0	0	00															
6	Accounts Payable							9	4	0	00										
7	Salaries Payable																				
8	J. Simpson, Capital						6	5	9	0	00										
9	J. Simpson, Drawing	2	0	0	0	00															
10	Income from Services							9	5	7	5	00									
11	Rent Expense		9	7	5	00															
12	Depr. Expense—Music Instruments																				
13	Salary Expense		8	5	0	00															
14	Utilities Expense		3	3	0	00															
15	Music Supplies Expense																				
16	Insurance Expense																				
17	Miscellaneous Expense			6	0	00															
18		17	1	0	5	00	17	1	0	5	00										

Practice Problem—Concluded

Simpson's Music Training

Work Sheet

For the Month Ended January 31, 200X

ADJUSTED TRIAL BALANCE		INCOME STATEMENT		BALANCE SHEET		
DEBIT	CREDIT	DEBIT	CREDIT	DEBIT	CREDIT	
						1
						2
						3
						4
						5
						6
						7
						8
						9
						10
						11
						12
						13
						14
						15
						16
						17
						18
						19
						20
						21
						22
						23
						24
						25
						26
						27
						28
						29
						30
						31
						32
						33

Problem 2—Preparation of Financial Statements Using a Work Sheet as a Guide

A partial work sheet for J.R. Ewing, Consulting is shown below.

J.R. Ewing, Consulting
Work Sheet (Partial)
For the Year Ended December 31, 200X

Account Title	Income Statement		Balance Sheet	
	Debit	Credit	Debit	Credit
Cash			22,170.00	
Office Supplies			810.00	
Prepaid Insurance			2,350.00	
Automobile			21,700.00	
Accum. Depr.—Automobile				9,000.00
Office Equipment			13,375.00	
Accumulated Depr.—Office Equip.				5,200.00
Accounts Payable				870.00
Salaries Payable				225.00
J.R. Ewing, Capital				69,460.00
J.R. Ewing, Drawing			48,000.00	
Professional Fees		115,900.00		
Rent Expense	18,000.00			
Office Supplies Expense	625.00			
Insurance Expense	1,500.00			
Salary Expense	64,700.00			
Telephone Expense	1,750.00			
Automobile Expense	1,100.00			
Depr. Expense—Automobile	3,000.00			
Depr. Expense—Office Equip.	1,200.00			
Miscellaneous Expense	375.00			
	92,250.00	115,900.00	108,405.00	84,755.00
Net Income	23,650.00			23,650.00
	115.900.00	115,900.00	108,405.00	108,405.00

Problem 2—Continued

Required:

1. Prepare an income statement for the year ended December 31, 200X. Arrange the expenses in the order of highest to lowest, with miscellaneous expense listed last.

3. Prepare a statement of owner's equity for the year ended December 31, 200X.

Problem 2—Concluded

3. Prepare a classified balance sheet as of December 31, 200X.

SOLUTIONS TO PRACTICE TEST

Part I	Part II	Part III
1. T	1. b	1. accounting cycle
2. F	2. d	2. interim financial statements
3. T	3. c	3. work sheet
4. F	4. d	4. adjusting entries
5. T	5. b	5. matching principle
6. T	6. c	6. income statement, balance sheet
7. F	7. d	7. depreciation
8. F	8. b	8. depreciable asset or long-term asset
9. T	9. c	9. contra-asset
10. F	10. a	10. book value

Part IV

Practice Problem 1

Simpson's Music Training
Work Sheet (Partial)
For the Month Ended January 31, 200X

Account Title	Trial Balance Debit	Trial Balance Credit	Adjustments Debit	Adjustments Credit
Cash	1,800.00			
Music Supplies	930.00			(a) 720.00
Prepaid Insurance	860.00			(b) 770.00
Musical Instruments	9,300.00			
Accum. Depr.—Music Instr.				(c) 900.00
Accounts Payable		940.00		
Salaries Payable				(d) 125.00
J. Simpson, Capital		6,590.00		
J. Simpson, Drawing	2,000.00			
Income from Services		9,575.00		
Rent Expense	975.00			
Depr. Expense—Music Instr.			(c) 900.00	
Salary Expense	850.00		(d) 125.00	
Utilities Expense	330.00			
Music Supplies Expense			(a) 720.00	
Insurance Expense			(b) 770.00	
Miscellaneous Expense	60.00			
	17,105.00	17,105.00	2,515.00	2,515.00

Practice Problem 1—Concluded

Simpson's Music Training
Work Sheet (Partial)
For the Month Ended January 31, 2000X

Account Title	Adjusted Trial Balance		Income Statement		Balance Sheet	
	Debit	Credit	Debit	Credit	Debit	Credit
Cash	1,800.00				1,800.00	
Music Supplies	210.00				210.00	
Prepaid Insurance	90.00				90.00	
Musical Instruments	9,300.00				9,300.00	
Accum. Depr.—Music Instr.		900.00				900.00
Accounts Payable		940.00				940.00
Salaries Payable		125.00				125.00
J. Simpson, Capital		6,590.00				6,590.00
J. Simpson, Drawing	2,000.00				2,000.00	
Income from Services		9,575.00		9,575.00		
Rent Expense	975.00		975.00			
Depr. Expense—Music Instr.			900.00			
Salary Expense	975.00		975.00			
Utilities Expense	330.00		330.00			
Music Supplies Expense	720.00		720.00			
Insurance Expense	770.00		770.00			
Miscellaneous Expense	60.00		60.00			
	18,130.00	18,130.00	4,730.00	9,575.00	13,400.00	8,555.00
Net Income			4,845.00			4,845.00
			9,575.00	9,575.00	13,400.00	13,400.00

Practice Problem 2

J.R. Ewing, Consulting
Income Statement
For the Year Ended December 31, 200X

Revenue:
    Professional Fees $115,900
Expenses:
    Salary Expense $64,700
    Rent Expense   18,000
    Depr. Expense—Automobile   3,000
    Telephone Expense   1,750
    Insurance Expense   1,500
    Depr. Expense—Office Equipment   1,200
    Automobile Expense   1,100
    Office Supplies Expense   625
    Miscellaneous Expense   375
      Total Expenses   92,250
Net Income $ 23,650

Practice Problem 2—Concluded

J.R. Ewing, Consulting
Statement of Owner's Equity
For the Year Ended December 31, 200X

J.R. Ewing, capital, January 1, 200X		$69,460
Net income for the year	$23,650	
Less withdrawals	48,000	
Net decrease in capital		(24,350)
J.R. Ewing, capital, December 31, 200X		$45,110

J.R. Ewing, Consulting
Balance Sheet
December 31, 200X

Assets

Current assets:		
Cash	$22,170	
Office supplies	810	
Prepaid insurance	2,350	
Total current assets		$25,330
Long-term assets:		
Automobile	$21,700	
Less accum. depr.—automobile	9,000 $12,700	
Office equipment	$13,375	
Less accum. Depr.—off. equip.	5,200 8,175	
Total long-term assets		20,875
Total assets		$46,205

Liabilities

Current liabilities:		
Accounts payable	$ 870	
Salaries payable	225	
Total current liabilities		$ 1,095

Owner's Equity

J.R. Ewing, capital		45,110
Total liabilities and owner's equity		$46,205

CHAPTER 3 WORKING PAPERS

EXERCISE 3A-1

1. _____
2. _____
3. _____
4. _____
5. _____
6. _____
7. _____
8. _____
9. _____

EXERCISE 3A-2

	Office Supplies			Office Supplies Expense
Unadjust. Bal.		(adj.)	(adj.)	
Ending Bal.				

EXERCISE 3A-3

	Depr. Expense Automobile		Accum. Depr.: Automobile
(adj.)		(adj.)	

EXERCISE 3A-4

	Depr. Exp: Medical Equip.		Accum. Depr.: Med. Equip.
(adj.)		(adj.)	

EXERCISE 3A-5

a.

Supplies	Supplies Expense

b.

Supplies	Supplies Expense

EXERCISE 3A-6

Salary Expense	Salaries Payable

EXERCISE 3A-7

	Income Statement		Balance Sheet	
	Debit	**Credit**	**Debit**	**Credit**
Net Income	_____	_____	_____	_____

EXERCISE 3A-8

	Income Statement		Balance Sheet	
	Debit	**Credit**	**Debit**	**Credit**
Net Loss	_____	_____	_____	_____

PROBLEM 3A-9

	Income Statement		Balance Sheet	
	Debit	**Credit**	**Debit**	**Credit**
Cash	_____	_____	_____	_____
Office Supplies	_____	_____	_____	_____
Office Equipment	_____	_____	_____	_____
Accum. Depr.—Office Equip.	_____	_____	_____	_____
Accounts Payable	_____	_____	_____	_____
Owner's Capital	_____	_____	_____	_____
Owner's Drawing	_____	_____	_____	_____
Professional Fees	_____	_____	_____	_____
Office Supplies Expense	_____	_____	_____	_____
Salary Expense	_____	_____	_____	_____

This page not used.

PROBLEM 3A-10
(Worksheet continues on facing page.)

Lee's Kitchen

Work Sheet

For the Month Ended June 30, 200X

	ACCOUNT TITLE	TRIAL BALANCE		ADJUSTMENTS	
		DEBIT	CREDIT	DEBIT	CREDIT
1	Cash	7 0 0 00			
2	Accounts Receivable	4 0 0 00			
3	Office Supplies	3 1 0 00			
4	Prepaid Insurance	6 8 0 00			
5	Kitchen Equipment	12 2 0 0 00			
6	Accum. Depr.—Kitchen Equipment				
7	Accounts Payable		6 0 0 00		
8	Salaries Payable				
9	J. Lee, Capital		14 3 2 5 00		
10	J. Lee, Drawing	3 0 0 0 00			
11	Income from Services		5 4 0 0 00		
12	Rent Expense	1 2 0 0 00			
13	Depr. Expense—Kitchen Equipment				
14	Salary Expense	1 4 0 0 00			
15	Utilities Expense	3 7 5 00			
16	Office Supplies Expense				
17	Insurance Expense				
18	Miscellaneous Expense	6 0 00			
19		20 3 2 5 00	20 3 2 5 00		

PROBLEM 3A-10—CONCLUDED
(Worksheet continues from facing page.)

Lee's Kitchen

Work Sheet

For the Month Ended June 30, 200X

ADJUSTED TRIAL BALANCE		INCOME STATEMENT		BALANCE SHEET	
DEBIT	CREDIT	DEBIT	CREDIT	DEBIT	CREDIT

PROBLEM 3A-11

| | Income Statement | | | Balance Sheet | |
	Debit	Credit		Debit	Credit
Cash	_____	_____		_____	_____
Accounts Receivable	_____	_____		_____	_____
Supplies	_____	_____		_____	_____
Automobile	_____	_____		_____	_____
Accum. Depr.—Auto	_____	_____		_____	_____
Salaries Payable	_____	_____		_____	_____
Owner's Capital	_____	_____		_____	_____
Owner's Drawing	_____	_____		_____	_____
Income from Services	_____	_____		_____	_____
Rent Expense	_____	_____		_____	_____
Utilities Expense	_____	_____		_____	_____

This page not used.

PROBLEM 3A-12
(Worksheet continues on facing page.)

Tony Mijares's Delivery Service

Work Sheet

For the Month Ended September 30, 200X

	ACCOUNT TITLE	TRIAL BALANCE		ADJUSTMENTS	
		DEBIT	CREDIT	DEBIT	CREDIT
1	Cash	5 6 0 0 00			
2	Accounts Receivable	9 0 0 00			
3	Office Supplies	8 0 0 00			
4	Prepaid Insurance	7 5 0 00			
5	Delivery Van	36 4 0 0 00			
6	Accum. Depr.—Delivery Van		4 2 0 0 00		
7	Accounts Payable		1 5 0 0 00		
8	Salaries Payable				
9	T. Mijares, Capital		26 4 5 0 00		
10	T. Mijares, Drawing	30 0 0 0 00			
11	Income from Services		106 1 0 0 00		
12	Rent Expense	35 0 0 0 00			
13	Depr. Expense—Delivery Van				
14	Salary Expense	24 4 0 0 00			
15	Utilities Expense	3 6 0 0 00			
16	Office Supplies Expense				
17	Insurance Expense				
18	Miscellaneous Expense	8 0 0 00			
19		138 2 5 0 00	138 2 5 0 00		
20					
21					
22					
23					
24					
25					
26					
27					
28					
29					
30					
31					
32					
33					

PROBLEM 3A-12—CONCLUDED

(Worksheet continues from facing page.)

Tony Mijares's Delivery Service

Work Sheet

For the Month Ended September 30, 200X

	ADJUSTED TRIAL BALANCE		INCOME STATEMENT		BALANCE SHEET		
	DEBIT	CREDIT	DEBIT	CREDIT	DEBIT	CREDIT	
							1
							2
							3
							4
							5
							6
							7
							8
							9
							10
							11
							12
							13
							14
							15
							16
							17
							18
							19
							20
							21
							22
							23
							24
							25
							26
							27
							28
							29
							30
							31
							32
							33

EXERCISE 3B-13

EXERCISE 3B-14

EXERCISE 3B-15

EXERCISE 3B-16

EXERCISE 3B-17

PROBLEM 3B-18

1.

2.

PROBLEM 3B-18—CONCLUDED

3.

PROBLEM 3B-19

1.

2.

PROBLEM 3B-19—CONCLUDED

3.

PROBLEM 3B-20

1.

2.

PROBLEM 3B-20—CONCLUDED

3.

PROBLEM 3B-21

1.

2.

PROBLEM 3B-21—CONCLUDED

3.

This page not used.

CHALLENGE PROBLEM
(Worksheet continues on facing page.)
2. and 3.

Judy Eary, CPA

Work Sheet

For the Month Ended December 31, 200X

	ACCOUNT TITLE	TRIAL BALANCE			ADJUSTMENTS			
		DEBIT	CREDIT		DEBIT		CREDIT	
1	Cash	31 6 3 0 00						
2	Office Supplies	3 2 4 0 00						
3	Prepaid Insurance	5 7 0 0 00						
4	Automobile	38 3 0 0 00						
5	Accum. Depr.—Automobile		9 6 0 0 00					
6	Office Equipment	36 4 0 0 00						
7	Accum. Depr.—Office Equipment		12 8 0 0 00					
8	Accounts Payable		6 4 1 0 00					
9	Salaries Payable							
10	J. Eary, Capital		86 2 5 5 00					
11	J. Eary, Drawing	60 0 0 0 00						
12	Professional Fees		194 0 0 0 00					
13	Rent Expense	31 0 0 0 00						
14	Office Supplies Expense							
15	Insurance Expense							
16	Salary Expense	88 0 0 0 00						
17	Telephone Expense	4 3 6 0 00						
18	Automobile Expense	3 1 5 5 00						
19	Depr. Expense—Automobile							
20	Depr. Expense—Office Equipment							
21	Charitable Contributions Expense	3 0 0 0 00						
22	Reference Library Expense	3 4 0 0 00						
23	Miscellaneous Expense	8 8 0 00						
24		309 0 6 5 00	309 0 6 5 00					
25								
26								
27								
28								
29								
30								
31								
32								

CHALLENGE PROBLEM

(Worksheet continues from facing page.)

2. and 3.

Judy Eary, CPA

Work Sheet

For the Month Ended December 31, 200X

ADJUSTED TRIAL BALANCE		INCOME STATEMENT		BALANCE SHEET		
DEBIT	CREDIT	DEBIT	CREDIT	DEBIT	CREDIT	
						1
						2
						3
						4
						5
						6
						7
						8
						9
						10
						11
						12
						13
						14
						15
						16
						17
						18
						19
						20
						21
						22
						23
						24
						25
						26
						27
						28
						29
						30
						31
						32

CHALLENGE PROBLEM—CONTINUED

3.

CHALLENGE PROBLEM—CONTINUED

4.

CHALLENGE PROBLEM—CONTINUED

5.

CHAPTER 4

ADJUSTING, CLOSING, AND REVERSING ENTRIES

PRACTICE TEST

Part I—True/False

Please circle the correct answer.

T F 1. An adjusting entry is a general journal entry to record an end-of-period adjustment to an account.

T F 2. Each adjusting entry affects only balance sheet accounts or only income statement accounts, but never both a balance sheet account and an income statement account within the same journal entry.

T F 3. Explanations are not needed for journalizing adjusting entries at the end of the accounting period.

T F 4. Closing entries are prepared before adjusting entries, but after the post-closing trial balance.

T F 5. Revenue, expense, and drawing accounts are temporary accounts that are closed at the end of the accounting period.

T F 6. Adjusting entries are posted to the general ledger immediately after they are recorded in the general journal.

T F 7. New balances in general ledger accounts are computed only once—at the end of the accounting period.

T F 8. Typically, the first step in closing would involve closing the drawing account.

T F 9. Closing entries in the general journal do not need to be posted to the general ledger.

T F 10. When closing entries are posted, temporary account balances will be zero.

Part II—Multiple Choice

Please circle the correct answer.

1. Which of these is a permanent account?
    a. The owner's capital account
    b. The owner's drawing account
    c. Professional Fees
    d. Rent Expense

2. The "Income Summary" account is which type of general ledger account?
    a. Asset
    b. Liability
    c. Owner's equity
    d. Revenue

3. Which of these would typically be the first closing entry?
    a. Close the drawing account
    b. Close the revenue account(s)
    c. Close the expense accounts
    d. Close the income summary account

Part II—Continued

4.   You know there is a net profit when
      a.   The income summary account has a debit balance.
      b.   The drawing account is credited to close it.
      c.   The owner's capital account is debited with the closing entry.
      d.   The income summary account has a credit balance.

5.   Which of these is a true statement about the post-closing trial balance?
      a.   It is a formal financial statement.
      b.   It is prepared after the adjusting entries have been posted to the general ledger.
      c.   It is prepared after the closing entries have been posted to the general ledger.
      d.   It is prepared the first day of the new accounting period.

6.   Adjusting entries are prepared, using the _____ columns of the work sheet as a guide.
      a.   Trial balance
      b.   Adjustments
      c.   Adjusted trial balance
      d.   Income statement

7.   New balances in all general ledger accounts after adjusting entries have been entered on the work sheet will be shown in the _____ columns of the work sheet.
      a.   Trial balance
      b.   Adjustments
      c.   Adjusted trial balance
      d.   Income statement

8.   Each account listed on the income statement is a(n) _____ account.
      a.   Balance sheet
      b.   Permanent
      c.   Temporary owner's equity
      d.   Capital

9.   Which of these is another synonym for "Income Summary" account?
      a.   Expense and Revenue Summary
      b.   Profit and Loss Summary
      c.   Income and Expense Summary
      d.   All of the above

10.   To close a revenue account, it is:
      a.   Debited
      b.   Credited
      c.   It is not closed.
      d.   None of the above

Part III—Fill in the Blank

1.   Adjusting entries are journalized using the _____ columns of the work sheet as a guide.

2.   The word "_____" appears in the item column of general ledger accounts when adjusting entries are posted.

3.   Revenue accounts, expense accounts, and the drawing account are known as _____ accounts.

4.   Asset, liabilities, and the owner's capital account are called _____ accounts; they all appear on the balance sheet.

Part III—Continued

5. The _____ is prepared after closing entries are journalized and posted, to check that the general ledger is still in balance.

6. The word "_____" appears in the item column of general ledger accounts when closing entries are posted.

7. After adjusting entries and closing entries are posted to general ledger accounts, new _____ are computed for each account.

8. The account(s) that is/are typically closed first is/are the _____ account(s).

9. The Income Summary account is a (temporary, permanent) account used for closing purposes.

10. To close the drawing account, you would (debit, credit) it.

Part IV—Practice Problems

Practice Problem 1—Adjusting Entries

Required:

Journalize adjusting entries for RDT Company which has the following adjustments for the year ended December 31, 200X:

a. Depreciation expense on equipment, $2,000.
b. Prepaid insurance that has expired, $800.
c. Accrued wages payable of $1,000.
d. Office supplies used during the year of $250.

GENERAL JOURNAL   PAGE

	DATE	DESCRIPTION	POST REF.	DEBIT	CREDIT	
1						1
2						2
3						3
4						4
5						5
6						6
7						7
8						8
9						9
10						10
11						11
12						12
13						13
14						14
15						15
16						16
17						17

Practice Problem 2—Closing Entries

Required:

Based on the adjusted trial balance for Roth Company shown below, prepare the closing entries.

Roth Company
Adjusted Trial Balance
December 31, 200X

	Debit	Credit
Cash	8,800	
Accounts Receivable	5,500	
Truck	6,000	
Accum. Depr.--Truck		3,000
Equipment	10,000	
Accum. Depr.--Equipment		4,200
Accounts Payable		2,500
Notes Payable		3,500
Jim Roth, Capital		14,700
Jim Roth, Drawing	5,000	
Service Revenue		22,000
Salary Expense	9,000	
Rent Expense	4,000	
Telephone Expense	800	
Repair Expense	500	
Miscellaneous Expense	300	
	49,900	49,900

GENERAL JOURNAL

PAGE

	DATE	DESCRIPTION	POST REF.	DEBIT	CREDIT	
1						1
2						2
3						3
4						4
5						5
6						6
7						7
8						8
9						9
10						10
11						11
12						12
13						13
14						14
15						15
16						16
17						17
18						18

SOLUTIONS TO PRACTICE TEST

Part I	Part II	Part III
1. T	1. a	1. adjustments
2. F	2. c	2. adjusting
3. T	3. b	3. temporary owner's equity
4. F	4. d	4. permanent
5. T	5. c	5. post-closing trial balance
6. T	6. b	6. closing
7. F	7. c	7. balances
8. F	8. c	8. revenue
9. F	9. d	9. temporary
10. T	10. a	10. credit

Part IV

Practice Problem 1

GENERAL JOURNAL   PAGE

DATE		DESCRIPTION	POST REF.	DEBIT	CREDIT
		Adjusting Entries			
200X					
Dec.	31	Depreciation Expense—Equipment		2,000	
		Accum. Depr.—Equipment			2,000
	31	Insurance Expense		800	
		Prepaid Insurance			800
	31	Wages Expense		1,000	
		Wages Payable			1,000
	31	Office Supplies Expense		250	
		Office Supplies			250

Practice Problem 2

	GENERAL JOURNAL			PAGE

DATE	DESCRIPTION	POST REF.	DEBIT	CREDIT
	Closing Entries			
200X				
Dec. 31	Service Revenue		22,000	
	Income Summary			22,000
31	Income Summary		14,600	
	Salary Expense			9,000
	Rent Expense			4,000
	Telephone Expense			800
	Repair Expense			500
	Miscellaneous Expense			300
31	Income Summary		7,400	
	Jim Roth, Capital			7,400
31	J. Arnold, Capital		5,000	
	Jim Roth, Drawing			5,000

CHAPTER 4 WORKING PAPERS

EXERCISE 4A-1

a.

b.

GENERAL JOURNAL   PAGE

	DATE		DESCRIPTION	POST REF.	DEBIT	CREDIT	
1							1
2							2
3							3

EXERCISE 4A-2

a.

b.

c.

GENERAL JOURNAL   PAGE

	DATE		DESCRIPTION	POST REF.	DEBIT	CREDIT	
1							1
2							2
3							3
4							4
5							5

EXERCISE 4A-3

a.

b.

GENERAL JOURNAL   PAGE

	DATE		DESCRIPTION	POST REF.	DEBIT	CREDIT	
1							1
2							2
3							3

EXERCISE 4A-4

a.

_____

_____

_____

_____

_____

_____

_____

b.   **GENERAL JOURNAL**   PAGE _____

	DATE		DESCRIPTION	POST REF.	DEBIT	CREDIT	
1							1
2							2
3							3

PROBLEM 4A-5

1.   **GENERAL JOURNAL**   PAGE 9

	DATE		DESCRIPTION	POST REF.	DEBIT	CREDIT	
1							1
2							2
3							3
4							4
5							5
6							6
7							7
8							8
9							9
10							10
11							11
12							12
13							13
14							14
15							15
16							16
17							17

PROBLEM 4A-5—CONTINUED
2. and 3.
General Ledger
ACCOUNT   Office Supplies   ACCOUNT NO. 121

DATE	ITEM	POST REF.	DEBIT	CREDIT	BALANCE	
					DEBIT	CREDIT

ACCOUNT   Prepaid Insurance   ACCOUNT NO. 131

DATE	ITEM	POST REF.	DEBIT	CREDIT	BALANCE	
					DEBIT	CREDIT

ACCOUNT   Accumulated Depreciation—Office Equipment   ACCOUNT NO. 141.1

DATE	ITEM	POST REF.	DEBIT	CREDIT	BALANCE	
					DEBIT	CREDIT

ACCOUNT   Accumulated Depreciation—Truck   ACCOUNT NO. 151.1

DATE	ITEM	POST REF.	DEBIT	CREDIT	BALANCE	
					DEBIT	CREDIT

ACCOUNT   Wages Payable   ACCOUNT NO. 221

DATE	ITEM	POST REF.	DEBIT	CREDIT	BALANCE	
					DEBIT	CREDIT

PROBLEM 4A-5—CONTINUED
2. and 3.

ACCOUNT   Wages Expense   ACCOUNT NO. 511

DATE	ITEM	POST REF.	DEBIT	CREDIT	BALANCE	
					DEBIT	CREDIT

ACCOUNT   Office Supplies Expense   ACCOUNT NO. 521

DATE	ITEM	POST REF.	DEBIT	CREDIT	BALANCE	
					DEBIT	CREDIT

ACCOUNT   Insurance Expense   ACCOUNT NO. 531

DATE	ITEM	POST REF.	DEBIT	CREDIT	BALANCE	
					DEBIT	CREDIT

ACCOUNT   Depreciation Expense—Office Equipment   ACCOUNT NO. 541

DATE	ITEM	POST REF.	DEBIT	CREDIT	BALANCE	
					DEBIT	CREDIT

ACCOUNT   Depreciation Expense—Truck   ACCOUNT NO. 551

DATE	ITEM	POST REF.	DEBIT	CREDIT	BALANCE	
					DEBIT	CREDIT

PROBLEM 4A-6

1.

Work Sheet

For the Year Ended December 31, 200X

	ACCOUNT TITLE	TRIAL BALANCE		ADJUSTMENTS		ADJ. TRIAL BALANCE		
		DEBIT	CREDIT	DEBIT	CREDIT	DEBIT	CREDIT	
3	Office Supplies	1 800 00						3
4	Prepaid Insurance	3 100 00						4
5	Office Equipment	10 200 00						5
6	Accum. Depr.: Office Equip.		3 800 00					6
7	Automobile	14 000 00						7
8	Accum. Depr.: Automobile		6 000 00					8
12	Wages Payable							12
15	Office Supplies Expense							15
16	Insurance Expense							16
17	Depr. Exp.: Office Equip.							17
18	Depr. Exp.: Automobile							18
19	Wages Expense							19
20								20
21								21
22								22
23								23
24								24
25								25
26								26
27								27
28								28
29								29
30								30
31								31
32								32
33								33

PROBLEM 4A-6—CONTINUED

2.   **GENERAL JOURNAL**   PAGE 11

	DATE	DESCRIPTION	POST REF.	DEBIT	CREDIT	
1						1
2						2
3						3
4						4
5						5
6						6
7						7
8						8
9						9
10						10
11						11
12						12
13						13
14						14
15						15

2.—4.

General Ledger
ACCOUNT   Office Supplies   ACCOUNT NO. 121

DATE	ITEM	POST REF.	DEBIT	CREDIT	BALANCE DEBIT	BALANCE CREDIT

ACCOUNT   Prepaid Insurance   ACCOUNT NO. 131

DATE	ITEM	POST REF.	DEBIT	CREDIT	BALANCE DEBIT	BALANCE CREDIT

ACCOUNT   Accumulated Depreciation—Office Equipment   ACCOUNT NO. 141.1

DATE	ITEM	POST REF.	DEBIT	CREDIT	BALANCE DEBIT	BALANCE CREDIT

PROBLEM 4A-6—CONTINUED
2.—4.

ACCOUNT   Accumulated Depreciation—Automobile   ACCOUNT NO. 142.1

DATE	ITEM	POST REF.	DEBIT	CREDIT	BALANCE DEBIT	BALANCE CREDIT

ACCOUNT   Wages Payable   ACCOUNT NO. 221

DATE	ITEM	POST REF.	DEBIT	CREDIT	BALANCE DEBIT	BALANCE CREDIT

ACCOUNT   Wages Expense   ACCOUNT NO. 511

DATE	ITEM	POST REF.	DEBIT	CREDIT	BALANCE DEBIT	BALANCE CREDIT

ACCOUNT   Office Supplies Expense   ACCOUNT NO. 521

DATE	ITEM	POST REF.	DEBIT	CREDIT	BALANCE DEBIT	BALANCE CREDIT

ACCOUNT   Insurance Expense   ACCOUNT NO. 531

DATE	ITEM	POST REF.	DEBIT	CREDIT	BALANCE DEBIT	BALANCE CREDIT

PROBLEM 4A-6—CONCLUDED

2.—4.

ACCOUNT   Depreciation Expense—Office Equipment   ACCOUNT NO. 541

DATE	ITEM	POST REF.	DEBIT	CREDIT	BALANCE	
					DEBIT	CREDIT

ACCOUNT   Depreciation Expense—Automobile   ACCOUNT NO. 542

DATE	ITEM	POST REF.	DEBIT	CREDIT	BALANCE	
					DEBIT	CREDIT

PROBLEM 4A-7

1.   **GENERAL JOURNAL**   PAGE 9

	DATE	DESCRIPTION	POST REF.	DEBIT	CREDIT	
1						1
2						2
3						3
4						4
5						5
6						6
7						7
8						8
9						9
10						10
11						11
12						12
13						13
14						14
15						15
16						16
17						17
18						18

PROBLEM 4A-7—CONTINUED
2. and 3.

General Ledger

ACCOUNT   Office Supplies   ACCOUNT NO. 121

DATE	ITEM	POST REF.	DEBIT	CREDIT	BALANCE DEBIT	BALANCE CREDIT

ACCOUNT   Prepaid Insurance   ACCOUNT NO. 131

DATE	ITEM	POST REF.	DEBIT	CREDIT	BALANCE DEBIT	BALANCE CREDIT

ACCOUNT   Accumulated Depreciation—Office Equipment   ACCOUNT NO. 141.1

DATE	ITEM	POST REF.	DEBIT	CREDIT	BALANCE DEBIT	BALANCE CREDIT

ACCOUNT   Accumulated Depreciation—Automobile   ACCOUNT NO. 151.1

DATE	ITEM	POST REF.	DEBIT	CREDIT	BALANCE DEBIT	BALANCE CREDIT

ACCOUNT   Wages Payable   ACCOUNT NO. 221

DATE	ITEM	POST REF.	DEBIT	CREDIT	BALANCE DEBIT	BALANCE CREDIT

PROBLEM 4A-7—CONCLUDED
2. and 3.

ACCOUNT   Wages Expense   ACCOUNT NO. 511

DATE	ITEM	POST REF.	DEBIT	CREDIT	BALANCE	
					DEBIT	CREDIT

ACCOUNT   Office Supplies Expense   ACCOUNT NO. 521

DATE	ITEM	POST REF.	DEBIT	CREDIT	BALANCE	
					DEBIT	CREDIT

ACCOUNT   Insurance Expense   ACCOUNT NO. 531

DATE	ITEM	POST REF.	DEBIT	CREDIT	BALANCE	
					DEBIT	CREDIT

ACCOUNT   Depreciation Expense—Office Equipment   ACCOUNT NO. 541

DATE	ITEM	POST REF.	DEBIT	CREDIT	BALANCE	
					DEBIT	CREDIT

ACCOUNT   Depreciation Expense—Truck   ACCOUNT NO. 551

DATE	ITEM	POST REF.	DEBIT	CREDIT	BALANCE	
					DEBIT	CREDIT

PROBLEM 4A-8

1.

Work Sheet

For the Year Ended December 31, 200X

	ACCOUNT TITLE	TRIAL BALANCE		ADJUSTMENTS		ADJ. TRIAL BALANCE		
		DEBIT	CREDIT	DEBIT	CREDIT	DEBIT	CREDIT	
3	Office Supplies	2 8 0 0 00						3
4	Prepaid Insurance	4 1 0 0 00						4
5	Office Equipment	8 2 0 0 00						5
6	Accum. Depr.: Office Equip.		2 4 0 0 00					6
7	Taxi	84 0 0 0 00						7
8	Accum. Depr.: Taxi		28 0 0 0 00					8
12	Wages Payable							12
15	Office Supplies Expense							15
16	Insurance Expense							16
17	Depr. Exp.: Office Equip.							17
18	Depr. Exp.: Taxi							18
19	Wages Expense							19
20								20
21								21
22								22
23								23
24								24
25								25
26								26
27								27
28								28
29								29
30								30
31								31
32								32
33								33

PROBLEM 4A-8—CONTINUED

2.   **GENERAL JOURNAL**   PAGE 11

	DATE	DESCRIPTION	POST REF.	DEBIT	CREDIT	
1						1
2						2
3						3
4						4
5						5
6						6
7						7
8						8
9						9
10						10
11						11
12						12
13						13
14						14
15						15

3. and 4.

General Ledger

ACCOUNT   Office Supplies   ACCOUNT NO. 121

DATE	ITEM	POST REF.	DEBIT	CREDIT	BALANCE DEBIT	BALANCE CREDIT

ACCOUNT   Prepaid Insurance   ACCOUNT NO. 131

DATE	ITEM	POST REF.	DEBIT	CREDIT	BALANCE DEBIT	BALANCE CREDIT

ACCOUNT   Accumulated Depreciation—Office Equipment   ACCOUNT NO. 141.1

DATE	ITEM	POST REF.	DEBIT	CREDIT	BALANCE DEBIT	BALANCE CREDIT

PROBLEM 4A-8—CONTINUED

3. and 4.

ACCOUNT Accumulated Depreciation—Taxi   ACCOUNT NO. 142.1

DATE		ITEM	POST REF.	DEBIT	CREDIT	BALANCE	
						DEBIT	CREDIT

ACCOUNT Wages Payable   ACCOUNT NO. 221

DATE		ITEM	POST REF.	DEBIT	CREDIT	BALANCE	
						DEBIT	CREDIT

ACCOUNT Wages Expense   ACCOUNT NO. 511

DATE		ITEM	POST REF.	DEBIT	CREDIT	BALANCE	
						DEBIT	CREDIT

ACCOUNT Office Supplies Expense   ACCOUNT NO. 521

DATE		ITEM	POST REF.	DEBIT	CREDIT	BALANCE	
						DEBIT	CREDIT

ACCOUNT Insurance Expense   ACCOUNT NO. 531

DATE		ITEM	POST REF.	DEBIT	CREDIT	BALANCE	
						DEBIT	CREDIT

PROBLEM 4A-8—CONCLUDED

3. and 4.

ACCOUNT   Depreciation Expense—Office Equipment   ACCOUNT NO. 541

DATE	ITEM	POST REF.	DEBIT	CREDIT	BALANCE	
					DEBIT	CREDIT

ACCOUNT   Depreciation Expense—Taxi   ACCOUNT NO. 542

DATE	ITEM	POST REF.	DEBIT	CREDIT	BALANCE	
					DEBIT	CREDIT

EXERCISE 4B-9

a.

b.   **GENERAL JOURNAL**   PAGE

	DATE	DESCRIPTION	POST REF.	DEBIT	CREDIT	
1						1
2						2
3						3
4						4
5						5

EXERCISE 4B-10

a.

b.   **GENERAL JOURNAL**   PAGE

	DATE	DESCRIPTION	POST REF.	DEBIT	CREDIT	
1						1
2						2
3						3
4						4
5						5

EXERCISE 4B-11

Post-Closing Trial Balance			

PROBLEM 4B-12

1.

GENERAL JOURNAL   PAGE 31

	DATE	DESCRIPTION	POST REF.	DEBIT	CREDIT	
1						1
2						2
3						3
4						4
5						5
6						6
7						7
8						8
9						9
10						10
11						11
12						12
13						13
14						14
15						15
16						16
17						17
18						18
19						19
20						20

PROBLEM 4B-12—CONTINUED

2. and 3.

General Ledger

ACCOUNT   Layla McLean, Capital   ACCOUNT NO. 311

DATE	ITEM	POST REF.	DEBIT	CREDIT	BALANCE	
					DEBIT	CREDIT
						4 7 8 3 0 00

ACCOUNT   Layla McLean, Drawing   ACCOUNT NO. 312

DATE	ITEM	POST REF.	DEBIT	CREDIT	BALANCE	
					DEBIT	CREDIT
					2 1 0 0 0 00	

ACCOUNT   Income Summary   ACCOUNT NO. 331

DATE	ITEM	POST REF.	DEBIT	CREDIT	BALANCE	
					DEBIT	CREDIT

ACCOUNT   Dry Cleaning Revenue   ACCOUNT NO. 411

DATE	ITEM	POST REF.	DEBIT	CREDIT	BALANCE	
					DEBIT	CREDIT
						4 6 0 0 0 00

ACCOUNT   Rent Expense   ACCOUNT NO. 511

DATE	ITEM	POST REF.	DEBIT	CREDIT	BALANCE	
					DEBIT	CREDIT
					2 2 0 0 0 00	

PROBLEM 4B-12—CONTINUED
2. and 3.

ACCOUNT   Salary Expense   ACCOUNT NO. 521

DATE	ITEM	POST REF.	DEBIT	CREDIT	BALANCE	
					DEBIT	CREDIT
200X					2 6 0 00	

ACCOUNT   Insurance Expense   ACCOUNT NO. 531

DATE	ITEM	POST REF.	DEBIT	CREDIT	BALANCE	
					DEBIT	CREDIT
200X.					4 0 0 00	

ACCOUNT   Supplies Expense   ACCOUNT NO. 533

DATE	ITEM	POST REF.	DEBIT	CREDIT	BALANCE	
					DEBIT	CREDIT
200X.					3 8 0 00	

ACCOUNT   Depreciation Expense—Office Equipment   ACCOUNT NO. 541

DATE	ITEM	POST REF.	DEBIT	CREDIT	BALANCE	
					DEBIT	CREDIT
200X.					1 2 0 0 00	

ACCOUNT   Depreciation Expense—Dry Cleaning Equipment   ACCOUNT NO. 545

DATE	ITEM	POST REF.	DEBIT	CREDIT	BALANCE	
					DEBIT	CREDIT
200X.					1 0 0 0 0 00	

PROBLEM 4B-12—CONCLUDED
2. and 3.

ACCOUNT   Repair Expense   ACCOUNT NO. 551

DATE	ITEM	POST REF.	DEBIT	CREDIT	BALANCE DEBIT	BALANCE CREDIT
					8 0 0 00	

ACCOUNT   Telephone Expense   ACCOUNT NO. 565

DATE	ITEM	POST REF.	DEBIT	CREDIT	BALANCE DEBIT	BALANCE CREDIT
					9 5 0 00	

ACCOUNT   Miscellaneous Expense   ACCOUNT NO. 599

DATE	ITEM	POST REF.	DEBIT	CREDIT	BALANCE DEBIT	BALANCE CREDIT
					6 0 0 00	

4.

Post-Closing Trial Balance

PROBLEM 4B-13

1.   **GENERAL JOURNAL**   PAGE 22

	DATE		DESCRIPTION	POST REF.	DEBIT	CREDIT	
1							1
2							2
3							3
4							4
5							5
6							6
7							7
8							8
9							9
10							10
11							11
12							12
13							13
14							14
15							15
16							16
17							17
18							18
19							19
20							20
21							21
22							22
23							23
24							24
25							25
26							26
27							27

2. and 3.

General Ledger

ACCOUNT   Jim Davis, Capital   ACCOUNT NO. 311

DATE	ITEM	POST REF.	DEBIT	CREDIT	BALANCE DEBIT	BALANCE CREDIT
						2 4 9 4 0 00

PROBLEM 4B-13—CONTINUED
2. and 3.

ACCOUNT   Jim Davis, Drawing   ACCOUNT NO. 312

DATE	ITEM	POST REF.	DEBIT	CREDIT	BALANCE DEBIT	BALANCE CREDIT
					5 0 0 0 0 00	

ACCOUNT   Income Summary   ACCOUNT NO. 331

DATE	ITEM	POST REF.	DEBIT	CREDIT	BALANCE DEBIT	BALANCE CREDIT

ACCOUNT   Professional Fees   ACCOUNT NO. 411

DATE	ITEM	POST REF.	DEBIT	CREDIT	BALANCE DEBIT	BALANCE CREDIT
						23 5 0 0 0 00

ACCOUNT   Rent Expense   ACCOUNT NO. 511

DATE	ITEM	POST REF.	DEBIT	CREDIT	BALANCE DEBIT	BALANCE CREDIT
					3 6 0 0 0 00	

ACCOUNT   Office Supplies Expense   ACCOUNT NO. 521

DATE	ITEM	POST REF.	DEBIT	CREDIT	BALANCE DEBIT	BALANCE CREDIT
					3 7 1 0 00	

PROBLEM 4B-13—CONTINUED
2. and 3.

ACCOUNT   Insurance Expense   ACCOUNT NO. 531

DATE	ITEM	POST REF.	DEBIT	CREDIT	BALANCE DEBIT	BALANCE CREDIT
					4 6 0 0 00	

ACCOUNT   Salary Expense   ACCOUNT NO. 541

DATE	ITEM	POST REF.	DEBIT	CREDIT	BALANCE DEBIT	BALANCE CREDIT
					9 2 9 0 0 00	

ACCOUNT   Telephone Expense   ACCOUNT NO. 545

DATE	ITEM	POST REF.	DEBIT	CREDIT	BALANCE DEBIT	BALANCE CREDIT
					3 8 5 0 00	

ACCOUNT   Automobile Expense   ACCOUNT NO. 548

DATE	ITEM	POST REF.	DEBIT	CREDIT	BALANCE DEBIT	BALANCE CREDIT
					2 8 5 0 00	

ACCOUNT   Depreciation Expense—Automobile   ACCOUNT NO. 551

DATE	ITEM	POST REF.	DEBIT	CREDIT	BALANCE DEBIT	BALANCE CREDIT
					7 3 5 0 00	

PROBLEM 4B-13—CONTINUED
2. and 3.

ACCOUNT   Depreciation Expense—Office Equipment   ACCOUNT NO. 555

DATE	ITEM	POST REF.	DEBIT	CREDIT	BALANCE	
					DEBIT	CREDIT
					4 6 0 0 00	

ACCOUNT   Charitable Contributions Expense   ACCOUNT NO. 561

DATE	ITEM	POST REF.	DEBIT	CREDIT	BALANCE	
					DEBIT	CREDIT
					3 5 0 0 00	

ACCOUNT   Miscellaneous Expense   ACCOUNT NO. 599

DATE	ITEM	POST REF.	DEBIT	CREDIT	BALANCE	
					DEBIT	CREDIT
					8 7 0 00	

4.

Post-Closing Trial Balance

PROBLEM 4B-14

1.

GENERAL JOURNAL

	DATE	DESCRIPTION	POST REF.	DEBIT	CREDIT	
1						1
2						2
3						3
4						4
5						5
6						6
7						7
8						8
9						9
10						10
11						11
12						12
13						13
14						14
15						15
16						16
17						17
18						18
19						19
20						20
21						21
22						22
23						23
24						24
25						25
26						26
27						27

2. and 3.

General Ledger

ACCOUNT   JoDell South, Capital   ACCOUNT NO. 311

DATE	ITEM	POST REF.	DEBIT	CREDIT	BALANCE	
					DEBIT	CREDIT
						3 7 4 3 0 00

PROBLEM 4B-14—CONTINUED
2. and 3.

ACCOUNT   JoDell South, Drawing   ACCOUNT NO. 312

DATE	ITEM	POST REF.	DEBIT	CREDIT	BALANCE DEBIT	BALANCE CREDIT
					1 1 0 0 0 00	

ACCOUNT   Income Summary   ACCOUNT NO. 331

DATE	ITEM	POST REF.	DEBIT	CREDIT	BALANCE DEBIT	BALANCE CREDIT

ACCOUNT   Consulting Fee Revenue   ACCOUNT NO. 411

DATE	ITEM	POST REF.	DEBIT	CREDIT	BALANCE DEBIT	BALANCE CREDIT
						2 6 0 0 0 00

ACCOUNT   Rent Expense   ACCOUNT NO. 511

DATE	ITEM	POST REF.	DEBIT	CREDIT	BALANCE DEBIT	BALANCE CREDIT
					1 2 0 0 0 00	

ACCOUNT   Salary Expense   ACCOUNT NO. 521

DATE	ITEM	POST REF.	DEBIT	CREDIT	BALANCE DEBIT	BALANCE CREDIT
					1 6 0 00	

PROBLEM 4B-14—CONTINUED
2. and 3.

ACCOUNT Insurance Expense   ACCOUNT NO. 531

DATE	ITEM	POST REF.	DEBIT	CREDIT	BALANCE	
					DEBIT	CREDIT
					6 0 0 00	

ACCOUNT Supplies Expense   ACCOUNT NO. 533

DATE	ITEM	POST REF.	DEBIT	CREDIT	BALANCE	
					DEBIT	CREDIT
					4 4 0 00	

ACCOUNT Depreciation Expense—Office Equipment   ACCOUNT NO. 541

DATE	ITEM	POST REF.	DEBIT	CREDIT	BALANCE	
					DEBIT	CREDIT
					9 0 0 00	

ACCOUNT Depreciation Expense—Automobile   ACCOUNT NO. 545

DATE	ITEM	POST REF.	DEBIT	CREDIT	BALANCE	
					DEBIT	CREDIT
					1 0 0 0 00	

ACCOUNT Repair Expense   ACCOUNT NO. 551

DATE	ITEM	POST REF.	DEBIT	CREDIT	BALANCE	
					DEBIT	CREDIT
					5 0 0 00	

PROBLEM 4B-14—CONTINUED
2. and 3.

ACCOUNT   Telephone Expense   ACCOUNT NO. 565

DATE	ITEM	POST REF.	DEBIT	CREDIT	BALANCE	
					DEBIT	CREDIT
					2 5 0 00	

ACCOUNT   Miscellaneous Expense   ACCOUNT NO. 599

DATE	ITEM	POST REF.	DEBIT	CREDIT	BALANCE	
					DEBIT	CREDIT
					6 0 0 00	

4.

Post-Closing Trial Balance

PROBLEM 4B-15

1.

GENERAL JOURNAL

PAGE 22

	DATE		DESCRIPTION	POST REF.	DEBIT	CREDIT	
1							1
2							2
3							3
4							4
5							5
6							6
7							7
8							8
9							9
10							10
11							11
12							12
13							13
14							14
15							15
16							16
17							17
18							18
19							19
20							20
21							21
22							22
23							23
24							24
25							25
26							26
27							27

2. and 3.

General Ledger

ACCOUNT   Phil Rogers, Capital   ACCOUNT NO. 311

DATE	ITEM	POST REF.	DEBIT	CREDIT	BALANCE	
					DEBIT	CREDIT
						1 0 3 9 5 00

PROBLEM 4B-15—CONTINUED
2. and 3.

ACCOUNT   Phil Rogers, Drawing   ACCOUNT NO. 312

DATE	ITEM	POST REF.	DEBIT	CREDIT	BALANCE DEBIT	BALANCE CREDIT
					3 5 0 0 0 00	

ACCOUNT   Income Summary   ACCOUNT NO. 331

DATE	ITEM	POST REF.	DEBIT	CREDIT	BALANCE DEBIT	BALANCE CREDIT

ACCOUNT   Professional Fees   ACCOUNT NO. 411

DATE	ITEM	POST REF.	DEBIT	CREDIT	BALANCE DEBIT	BALANCE CREDIT
						19 7 0 0 0 00

ACCOUNT   Rent Expense   ACCOUNT NO. 511

DATE	ITEM	POST REF.	DEBIT	CREDIT	BALANCE DEBIT	BALANCE CREDIT
					3 3 0 0 0 00	

ACCOUNT   Office Supplies Expense   ACCOUNT NO. 521

DATE	ITEM	POST REF.	DEBIT	CREDIT	BALANCE DEBIT	BALANCE CREDIT
					1 8 0 0 00	

PROBLEM 4B-15—CONTINUED
2. and 3.

ACCOUNT   Insurance Expense   ACCOUNT NO. 531

DATE	ITEM	POST REF.	DEBIT	CREDIT	BALANCE	
					DEBIT	CREDIT
					4 1 0 0 00	

ACCOUNT   Salary Expense   ACCOUNT NO. 541

DATE	ITEM	POST REF.	DEBIT	CREDIT	BALANCE	
					DEBIT	CREDIT
					6 2 2 0 0 00	

ACCOUNT   Telephone Expense   ACCOUNT NO. 545

DATE	ITEM	POST REF.	DEBIT	CREDIT	BALANCE	
					DEBIT	CREDIT
					3 2 7 5 00	

ACCOUNT   Automobile Expense   ACCOUNT NO. 548

DATE	ITEM	POST REF.	DEBIT	CREDIT	BALANCE	
					DEBIT	CREDIT
					3 2 9 0 00	

ACCOUNT   Depreciation Expense—Automobile   ACCOUNT NO. 551

DATE	ITEM	POST REF.	DEBIT	CREDIT	BALANCE	
					DEBIT	CREDIT
					5 1 4 0 00	

PROBLEM 4B-15—CONTINUED

2. and 3.

ACCOUNT   Depreciation Expense—Office Equipment   ACCOUNT NO. 555

DATE	ITEM	POST REF.	DEBIT	CREDIT	BALANCE DEBIT	BALANCE CREDIT
					3 8 2 0 00	

ACCOUNT   Charitable Contributions Expense   ACCOUNT NO. 561

DATE	ITEM	POST REF.	DEBIT	CREDIT	BALANCE DEBIT	BALANCE CREDIT
					4 0 0 0 00	

ACCOUNT   Miscellaneous Expense   ACCOUNT NO. 599

DATE	ITEM	POST REF.	DEBIT	CREDIT	BALANCE DEBIT	BALANCE CREDIT
					9 2 0 00	

4.

Post-Closing Trial Balance

EXERCISE 4C-16

_____   Depreciation Expense debit, Accumulated Depreciation credit

_____   Insurance Expense debit, Prepaid Insurance credit

_____   Wages Expense debit, Wages Payable credit

_____   Supplies Expense debit, Supplies credit

EXERCISE 4C-17

Step No.	Accounting Cycle Steps
_____	_____
_____	_____
_____	_____
_____	_____
_____	_____
_____	_____
_____	_____
_____	_____
_____	_____

PROBLEM 4C-18

1.   **GENERAL JOURNAL**   PAGE 1

	DATE	DESCRIPTION	POST REF.	DEBIT	CREDIT	
1						1
2						2
3						3

2.   **GENERAL JOURNAL**   PAGE 1

	DATE	DESCRIPTION	POST REF.	DEBIT	CREDIT	
1						1
2						2
3						3

3.   **GENERAL JOURNAL**   PAGE 1

	DATE	DESCRIPTION	POST REF.	DEBIT	CREDIT	
1						1
2						2
3						3

PROBLEM 4C-18—CONCLUDED

4.

General Ledger

ACCOUNT   Wage Expense   ACCOUNT NO. 511

DATE	ITEM	POST REF.	DEBIT	CREDIT	BALANCE	
					DEBIT	CREDIT
					2 5 0 0 0 00	

ACCOUNT   Wages Payable   ACCOUNT NO. 221

DATE	ITEM	POST REF.	DEBIT	CREDIT	BALANCE	
					DEBIT	CREDIT

5.   **GENERAL JOURNAL**   PAGE 1

	DATE	DESCRIPTION	POST REF.	DEBIT	CREDIT	
1						1
2						2
3						3

PROBLEM 4C-19   **GENERAL JOURNAL**   PAGE 1

	DATE	DESCRIPTION	POST REF.	DEBIT	CREDIT	
1						1
2						2
3						3
4						4
5						5
6						6
7						7
8						8
9						9
10						10
11						11
12						12

PROBLEM 4C-20

1.   **GENERAL JOURNAL**   PAGE 1

	DATE		DESCRIPTION	POST REF.	DEBIT	CREDIT	
1							1
2							2
3							3

2.   **GENERAL JOURNAL**   PAGE 1

	DATE		DESCRIPTION	POST REF.	DEBIT	CREDIT	
1							1
2							2
3							3

3.   **GENERAL JOURNAL**   PAGE 1

	DATE		DESCRIPTION	POST REF.	DEBIT	CREDIT	
1							1
2							2
3							3

4.

General Ledger
ACCOUNT   Wage Expense   ACCOUNT NO. 511

DATE	ITEM	POST REF.	DEBIT	CREDIT	BALANCE	
					DEBIT	CREDIT
					3 8 0 0 0 00	

ACCOUNT   Wages Payable   ACCOUNT NO. 221

DATE	ITEM	POST REF.	DEBIT	CREDIT	BALANCE	
					DEBIT	CREDIT

PROBLEM 4C-20—CONCLUDED
5.   **GENERAL JOURNAL**   PAGE 1

	DATE		DESCRIPTION	POST REF.	DEBIT	CREDIT	
1							1
2							2
3							3
4							4

PROBLEM 4C-21
1., 2., and 3.
GENERAL JOURNAL   PAGE 11

	DATE		DESCRIPTION	POST REF.	DEBIT	CREDIT	
1							1
2							2
3							3
4							4
5							5
6							6
7							7
8							8
9							9
10							10
11							11
12							12
13							13
14							14
15							15
16							16
17							17
18							18
19							19
20							20
21							21
22							22
23							23
24							24
25							25
26							26
27							27

This page not used.

CHALLENGE PROBLEM

1.

Work Sheet

	ACCOUNT TITLE	TRIAL BALANCE										ADJUSTMENTS								
		DEBIT					CREDIT					DEBIT					CREDIT			
1	Cash	11	2	0	0	00														
2	Office Supplies		8	0	0	00														
3	Prepaid Insurance	2	8	0	0	00														
4	Automobile	15	0	0	0	00														
5	Accum. Depreciation—Automobile						3	0	0	0	00									
6	Office Equipment	12	0	0	0	00														
7	Accum. Depr.—Office Equipment						4	0	0	0	00									
8	Accounts Payable						2	1	0	0	00									
9	Wages Payable																			
10	Cindy Moats, Capital						22	0	0	0	00									
11	Cindy Moats, Drawing	9	0	0	0	00														
12	Professional Fees						58	0	0	0	00									
13	Rent Expense	9	2	0	0	00														
14	Wages Expense	22	0	0	0	00														
15	Office Supplies Expense																			
16	Insurance Expense																			
17	Telephone Expense	1	8	0	0	00														
18	Automobile Repair Expense		9	0	0	00														
19	Depr. Expense—Automobile																			
20	Depr. Exp.—Office Equipment																			
21	Charitable Contributions Expense	1	1	0	0	00														
22	Professional Development Exp.	3	0	0	0	00														
23	Miscellaneous Expense		3	0	0	00														
24																				
25	Net Income	89	1	0	0	00	89	1	0	0	00									
26																				
27																				
28																				
29																				
30																				
31																				
32																				
33																				

CHALLENGE PROBLEM—CONCLUDED

1.

ADJUSTED TRIAL BALANCE		INCOME STATEMENT		BALANCE SHEET		
DEBIT	CREDIT	DEBIT	CREDIT	DEBIT	CREDIT	
						1
						2
						3
						4
						5
						6
						7
						8
						9
						10
						11
						12
						13
						14
						15
						16
						17
						18
						19
						20
						21
						22
						23
						24
						25
						26
						27
						28
						29
						30
						31
						32
						33

CHALLENGE PROBLEM—CONTINUED

2.   **GENERAL JOURNAL**   PAGE 21

	DATE		DESCRIPTION	POST REF.	DEBIT	CREDIT	
1			Adjusting Entries				1
2							2
3							3
4							4
5							5
6							6
7							7
8							8
9							9
10							10
11							11
12							12
13							13
14							14
15							15
16							16
17							17
18							18
19							19
20							20
21							21
22							22
23							23
24							24
25							25
26							26
27							27
28							28
29							29
30							30
31							31
32							32
33							33
34							34
35							35
36							36

CHALLENGE PROBLEM—CONTINUED

3.   **GENERAL JOURNAL**   PAGE 22

	DATE		DESCRIPTION	POST REF.	DEBIT	CREDIT	
1			Closing Entries				1
2							2
3							3
4							4
5							5
6							6
7							7
8							8
9							9
10							10
11							11
12							12
13							13
14							14
15							15
16							16
17							17
18							18
19							19
20							20
21							21
22							22
23							23
24							24
25							25
26							26
27							27
28							28
29							29
30							30
31							31
32							32
33							33
34							34
35							35
36							36

CHALLENGE PROBLEM—CONTINUED

4.   **GENERAL JOURNAL**

	DATE		DESCRIPTION	POST REF.	DEBIT	CREDIT	
1			Reversing Entry				1
2							2
3							3
4							4
5							5
6							6
7							7
8							8
9							9
10							10
11							11
12							12
13							13
14							14
15							15
16							16
17							17
18							18
19							19
20							20
21							21
22							22
23							23
24							24
25							25
26							26
27							27
28							28
29							29
30							30
31							31
32							32
33							33
34							34
35							35
36							36

COMPREHENSIVE REVIEW PROBLEM 2

Turner Repair Service
Chart of Accounts

Assets:

Cash	111
Accounts Receivable	118
Office Supplies	121
Prepaid Insurance	131
Office Equipment	141
Accum. Depr.—Office Equipment	141.1
Truck	211
Accum. Depr.—Truck	151.1

Liabilities:

Accounts Payable	211
Notes Payable	221
Wages Payable	231

Owner's Equity:

Bonnie Turner, Capital	311
Bonnie Turner, Drawing	312
Income Summary	331

Revenue:

Delivery Fees	411

Expenses:

Wages Expense	511
Rent Expense	521
Insurance Expense	522
Office Supplies Expense	531
Depr. Expense—Equipment	541
Depr. Expense—Truck	545
Repairs Expense	551
Telephone Expense	555
Utilities Expense	565
Advertising Expense	575
Miscellaneous Expense	599

COMPREHENSIVE REVIEW PROBLEM 2

2.

GENERAL JOURNAL

PAGE 22

	DATE	DESCRIPTION	POST REF.	DEBIT	CREDIT	
1						1
2						2
3						3
4						4
5						5
6						6
7						7
8						8
9						9
10						10
11						11
12						12
13						13
14						14
15						15
16						16
17						17
18						18
19						19
20						20
21						21
22						22
23						23
24						24
25						25
26						26
27						27
28						28
29						29
30						30
31						31
32						32
33						33
34						34
35						35
36						36

COMPREHENSIVE REVIEW PROBLEM 2

2.

GENERAL JOURNAL

PAGE 23

	DATE	DESCRIPTION	POST REF.	DEBIT	CREDIT	
1						1
2						2
3						3
4						4
5						5
6						6
7						7
8						8
9						9
10						10
11						11
12						12
13						13
14						14
15						15
16						16
17						17
18						18
19						19
20						20
21						21
22						22
23						23
24						24
25						25
26						26
27						27
28						28
29						29
30						30
31						31
32						32
33						33
34						34
35						35
36						36

COMPREHENSIVE REVIEW PROBLEM 2

2.

GENERAL JOURNAL

	DATE		DESCRIPTION	POST REF.	DEBIT	CREDIT	
1							1
2							2
3							3
4							4
5							5
6							6
7							7
8							8
9							9
10							10
11							11
12							12
13							13
14							14
15							15
16							16
17							17
18							18
19							19
20							20
21							21
22							22
23							23
24							24
25							25
26							26
27							27
28							28
29							29
30							30
31							31
32							32
33							33
34							34
35							35

COMPREHENSIVE REVIEW PROBLEM 2
7.

GENERAL JOURNAL

PAGE 25

	DATE		DESCRIPTION	POST REF.	DEBIT	CREDIT	
1							1
2							2
3							3
4							4
5							5
6							6
7							7
8							8
9							9
10							10
11							11
12							12
13							13
14							14
15							15
16							16
17							17
18							18
19							19
20							20
21							21
22							22
23							23
24							24
25							25
26							26
27							27
28							28
29							29
30							30
31							31
32							32
33							33
34							34
35							35

COMPREHENSIVE REVIEW PROBLEM 2
1. and 3.

ACCOUNT   Cash   ACCOUNT NO. 111

DATE	ITEM	POST REF.	DEBIT	CREDIT	BALANCE	
					DEBIT	CREDIT

ACCOUNT   Accounts Receivable   ACCOUNT NO. 118

DATE	ITEM	POST REF.	DEBIT	CREDIT	BALANCE	
					DEBIT	CREDIT

ACCOUNT   Office Supplies   ACCOUNT NO. 121

DATE	ITEM	POST REF.	DEBIT	CREDIT	BALANCE	
					DEBIT	CREDIT

COMPREHENSIVE REVIEW PROBLEM 2—CONTINUED
1. and 3.

ACCOUNT   Prepaid Insurance   ACCOUNT NO. 131

DATE	ITEM	POST REF.	DEBIT	CREDIT	BALANCE DEBIT	BALANCE CREDIT

ACCOUNT   Office Equipment   ACCOUNT NO. 141

DATE	ITEM	POST REF.	DEBIT	CREDIT	BALANCE DEBIT	BALANCE CREDIT

ACCOUNT   Accumulated Depreciation—Office Equipment   ACCOUNT NO. 141.1

DATE	ITEM	POST REF.	DEBIT	CREDIT	BALANCE DEBIT	BALANCE CREDIT

ACCOUNT   Truck   ACCOUNT NO. 151

DATE	ITEM	POST REF.	DEBIT	CREDIT	BALANCE DEBIT	BALANCE CREDIT

ACCOUNT   Accumulated Depreciation—Truck   ACCOUNT NO. 151.1

DATE	ITEM	POST REF.	DEBIT	CREDIT	BALANCE DEBIT	BALANCE CREDIT

COMPREHENSIVE REVIEW PROBLEM 2—CONTINUED
1. and 3.

ACCOUNT Accounts Payable   ACCOUNT NO. 211

DATE	ITEM	POST REF.	DEBIT	CREDIT	BALANCE	
					DEBIT	CREDIT

ACCOUNT Notes Payable   ACCOUNT NO. 221

DATE	ITEM	POST REF.	DEBIT	CREDIT	BALANCE	
					DEBIT	CREDIT

ACCOUNT Wages Payable   ACCOUNT NO. 231

DATE	ITEM	POST REF.	DEBIT	CREDIT	BALANCE	
					DEBIT	CREDIT

ACCOUNT Bonnie Turner, Capital   ACCOUNT NO. 311

DATE	ITEM	POST REF.	DEBIT	CREDIT	BALANCE	
					DEBIT	CREDIT

ACCOUNT Bonnie Turner, Drawing   ACCOUNT NO. 312

DATE	ITEM	POST REF.	DEBIT	CREDIT	BALANCE	
					DEBIT	CREDIT

COMPREHENSIVE REVIEW PROBLEM 2—CONTINUED

1. and 3.

ACCOUNT   Income Summary   ACCOUNT NO. 331

DATE	ITEM	POST REF.	DEBIT	CREDIT	BALANCE DEBIT	BALANCE CREDIT

ACCOUNT   Repair Fees   ACCOUNT NO. 411

DATE	ITEM	POST REF.	DEBIT	CREDIT	BALANCE DEBIT	BALANCE CREDIT

ACCOUNT   Wages Expense   ACCOUNT NO. 511

DATE	ITEM	POST REF.	DEBIT	CREDIT	BALANCE DEBIT	BALANCE CREDIT

ACCOUNT   Rent Expense   ACCOUNT NO. 521

DATE	ITEM	POST REF.	DEBIT	CREDIT	BALANCE DEBIT	BALANCE CREDIT

COMPREHENSIVE REVIEW PROBLEM 2—CONTINUED
1. and 3.

ACCOUNT   Insurance Expense   ACCOUNT NO. 522

DATE	ITEM	POST REF.	DEBIT	CREDIT	BALANCE DEBIT	BALANCE CREDIT

ACCOUNT   Office Supplies Expense   ACCOUNT NO. 531

DATE	ITEM	POST REF.	DEBIT	CREDIT	BALANCE DEBIT	BALANCE CREDIT

ACCOUNT   Depreciation Expense—Equipment   ACCOUNT NO. 541

DATE	ITEM	POST REF.	DEBIT	CREDIT	BALANCE DEBIT	BALANCE CREDIT

ACCOUNT   Depreciation Expense—Truck   ACCOUNT NO. 545

DATE	ITEM	POST REF.	DEBIT	CREDIT	BALANCE DEBIT	BALANCE CREDIT

ACCOUNT   Repair Expense   ACCOUNT NO. 551

DATE	ITEM	POST REF.	DEBIT	CREDIT	BALANCE DEBIT	BALANCE CREDIT

COMPREHENSIVE REVIEW PROBLEM 2—CONTINUED
1. and 3.

ACCOUNT   Telephone Expense   ACCOUNT NO. 555

DATE	ITEM	POST REF.	DEBIT	CREDIT	BALANCE	
					DEBIT	CREDIT

ACCOUNT   Utilities Expense   ACCOUNT NO. 565

DATE	ITEM	POST REF.	DEBIT	CREDIT	BALANCE	
					DEBIT	CREDIT

ACCOUNT   Advertising Expense   ACCOUNT NO. 575

DATE	ITEM	POST REF.	DEBIT	CREDIT	BALANCE	
					DEBIT	CREDIT

ACCOUNT   Miscellaneous Expense   ACCOUNT NO. 599

DATE	ITEM	POST REF.	DEBIT	CREDIT	BALANCE	
					DEBIT	CREDIT

COMPREHENSIVE REVIEW PROBLEM 2—CONTINUED

(Continued on facing page)

1.

	Work Sheet					
	For the Month Ended January 31, 200X					
ACCOUNT TITLE	TRIAL BALANCE		ADJUSTMENTS			
	DEBIT	CREDIT	DEBIT	CREDIT		
1 Cash						
2 Accounts Receivable						
3 Office Supplies						
4 Prepaid Insurance						
5 Office Equipment						
6 Accum. Depr.—Office Equipment						
7 Truck						
8 Accum. Depr.—Truck						
9 Accounts Payable						
10 Notes Payable						
11 Wages Payable						
12 Bonnie Turner, Capital						
13 Bonnie Turner, Drawing						
14 Repair Fees						
15 Wage Expense						
16 Rent Expense						
17 Insurance Expense						
18 Office Supplies Expense						
19 Depr. Exp.—Equipment						
20 Depr. Exp.—Truck						
21 Repair Expense						
22 Telephone Expense						
23 Utilities Expense						
24 Advertising Expense						
25 Miscellaneous Expense						
26						
27						
28						
29						
30						
31						
32						

COMPREHENSIVE REVIEW PROBLEM 2—CONTINUED

(Continued from facing page)

1.

ADJUSTED TRIAL BALANCE		INCOME STATEMENT		BALANCE SHEET		
DEBIT	CREDIT	DEBIT	CREDIT	DEBIT	CREDIT	
						1
						2
						3
						4
						5
						6
						7
						8
						9
						10
						11
						12
						13
						14
						15
						16
						17
						18
						19
						20
						21
						22
						23
						24
						25
						26
						27
						28
						29
						30
						31
						32
						33

COMPREHENSIVE REVIEW PROBLEM 2—CONTINUED

5.

Income Statement

5.

Statement of Owner's Equity

COMPREHENSIVE REVIEW PROBLEM 2—CONCLUDED

5.

Balance Sheet					

COMPREHENSIVE REVIEW PROBLEM 2—CONCLUDED

8.

Post-Closing Trial Balance		

CHAPTER 5

ACCOUNTING FOR CASH

PRACTICE TEST

Part I—True/False

Please circle the correct answer.

T F 1.   Internal control involves methods designed to safeguard assets.

T F 2.   The revenue account title "Income from Services" should be credited for the actual cash count, when comparing the cash register tape to the cash collected.

T F 3.   A change fund is a convenient way to pay for small items without the necessity of writing business checks for small dollar amounts.

T F 4.   A change fund should always be deducted from the actual cash count before comparing the cash register tape to the amount of cash counted.

T F 5.   A petty cash fund is used for those customers or clients who do not have the exact amount of change.

T F 6.   When replenishing the petty cash fund, the account "Petty Cash" should be debited and cash credited from the necessary dollar amount to replenish the fund.

T F 7.   The drawee is the depositor who orders the bank to pay cash.

T F 8.   The payee is the person being paid the cash.

T F 9.   Deposits in transit are deducted from the bank statement balance.

T F 10. All additions and deductions to either the book balance or the bank statement balance must be journalized.

Part II—Multiple Choice

Please circle the correct answer.

1.   Cash items include
   a.   Checks
   b.   Credit card receipts
   c.   Money orders
   d.   All the above

2.   Methods designed by management to safeguard assets are called
   a.   Quality control
   b.   Internal security
   c.   Internal control
   d.   Entrapment

3.   The actual cash count for the day is $1,825.45. The cash register tape indicates sales for the day were $1,826.55. The journal entry would include a
   a.   Debit to Cash for $1,826.55
   b.   Credit to Income from Services for $1,825.45
   c.   Credit to Cash Short and Over for $1.10
   d.   Debit to Cash Short and Over for $1.10

Part II—Continued

4.　　　A change fund has been established for $200. The actual cash count, including the change fund is $3,467.89. The cash register tape indicates sales for the day were $3,265.59. The journal entry would include a
　　　a.　Debit to Cash Short and Over for $202.30
　　　b.　Credit to Cash Short and Over for $202.30
　　　c.　Credit to Income from Services for $3,467.89
　　　d.　Credit to Cash Short and Over for $2.30

5.　　　The petty cash fund was originally set up for $100. Petty cash vouchers total $91. There is $7 remaining in the fund. The proper journal entry to replenish the petty cash fund would include a
　　　a.　Debit to Petty Cash Fund for $91
　　　b.　Credit to Petty Cash Fund for $93
　　　c.　Debit to Cash Short and Over for $2
　　　d.　Credit to Cash for $91

6.　　　The type of endorsement where the depositor simply signs his or her name on the bank of the check is called a
　　　a.　Blank endorsement
　　　b.　Restrictive endorsement
　　　c.　Controlled endorsement
　　　d.　Name endorsement

7.　　　The bank on which the check is drawn is called the
　　　a.　Drawer
　　　b.　Drawee
　　　c.　Payee
　　　d.　Bankee

8.　　　In a bank reconciliation, outstanding checks should be
　　　a.　Added to the checkbook balance
　　　b.　Deducted from the checkbook balance
　　　c.　Added to the bank statement balance
　　　d.　Deducted from the bank statement balance

9.　　　An NSF check for $200 was included with the monthly bank statement. The proper journal entry to record the NSF check would include a
　　　a.　Debit to NSF check expense
　　　b.　Debit to Cash for $200
　　　c.　Debit to Accounts Receivable for $200
　　　d.　Debit to Miscellaneous Expense for $200

10.　　　Included with the monthly bank statement is a credit memo representing a bank collection of a note. The principle was $4,000 and the interest earned was $65. The proper journal entry would include a
　　　a.　Debit to Notes Receivable for $4,000
　　　b.　Credit to Cash for $4,065
　　　c.　Credit to Notes Receivable for $4,065
　　　d.　Credit to Interest Earned for $65

Part III—Fill in the Blank

1.　　　Cash and cash items received by a business are known as _____.

2.　　　A special ledger account called _____ is used to keep track of daily shortages and overages of cash.

Part III—Concluded

3.   Always credit the account _____ for the amount that appears on the cash register tape and debit the account _____ for the actual cash count.

4.   Most businesses like to start off the day with a _____ for those customers or clients who do not have the exact amount of change.

5.   Sometimes it is convenient to pay for small items using an office fund known as a _____.

6.   When a petty cash fund is maintained, it is good practice to keep a formal record of all payments from the fund. A special multi-column form, known as a _____, is used.

7.   When the depositor adds words such as "For Deposit Only" on the back of the check, we call this a _____ endorsement.

8.   When the depositor simply signs his or her name on the back of the check, we call this a _____ endorsement.

9.   In a bank reconciliation, outstanding checks are _____ (to or from) the bank statement and deposits in transit are _____ (to or from) the bank statement.

10.   In a bank reconciliation, journal entries are prepared for all additions and/or deductions made to the _____.

Part IV—Practice Problems

Practice Problem 1—Replenishing a Petty Cash Fund

A petty cash fund was established for $150 on March 1. The following payments were made from the fund during March.

Automobile Expense ....$ 58.25
Miscellaneous Expense.. 33.18
Postage Expense 29.00
Supplies Expense 17.45
Telephone Expense 8.30
$146.18

There is $1.12 remaining in the petty cash fund on March 31.

Required:
1.   Prepare the journal entry to establish the petty cash fund on March 1.
2.   Prepare the journal enry to replenish the fund on March 31. Omit explanations

Practice Problem 1—Concluded

GENERAL JOURNAL

PAGE ___

	DATE		DESCRIPTION	POST REF.	DEBIT	CREDIT	
1							1
2							2
3							3
4							4
5							5
6							6
7							7
8							8
9							9
10							10
11							11
12							12
13							13

Practice Problem 2—Reconciling a Bank Statement and Preparing Journal Entries

Johnson Company has an ending balance in their checking account, as of November 30, of $8,506.05. On the same date, the bank statement shows an ending balance of $12,735.00. The following information is discovered by comparing checks deposited and written, noting service fees, and reading other debit and credit memos appearing with the bank statement.

Deposits in transit:	11/29	$475.00
	11/30	960.00

Outstanding checks:	No. 7246	$ 99.45
	No. 7253	512.50
	No. 7258	183.00

Debit memos:		
Bank service charge:		15.00
NSF check:		325.00

Credit memo: Note receivable collected by the bank.

	Principal:	5,000.00
	Interest Earned:	200.00

Error on check no. 7233: Check was written correctly for $67 for office supplies. Check was incorrectly recorded as $76.

Practice Problem 2—Concluded

Required:

1.   Prepare a bank reconciliation as of November 30, 200X
2.   Prepare the required journal entries. Omit explanations.

Johnson Company
Bank Reconciliation
November 30, 200X

Bank statement balance, November 30 .... $ _____
Add: .... _____

     Subtotal .... _____   _____
Deduct:... _____

            _____   _____
Adjusted bank balance .... _____

Ending check book balance, November 30 .... $ _____
Add: .... _____
            _____
     Subtotal .... _____   _____
Deduct:... _____

Adjusted bank balance .... _____

GENERAL JOURNAL   PAGE

	DATE	DESCRIPTION	POST REF.	DEBIT	CREDIT	
1						1
2						2
3						3
4						4
5						5
6						6
7						7
8						8
9						9
10						10
11						11
12						12
13						13
14						14
15						15

SOLUTIONS TO PRACTICE TEST

Part I	Part II	Part III
1. T	1. d	1. cash receipts
2. F	2. c	2. cash short and over
3. F	3. d	3. Income from Services, Cash
4. T	4. d	4. change fund
5. F	5. c	5. petty cash fund
6. F	6. a	6. petty cash payments record
7. F	7. b	7. restricted
8. T	8. d	8. blank
9. F	9. c	9. deducted from, added to
10. F	10. d	10. check book balance

Part IV

Practice Problem 1

(1)   Mar. 1   Petty Cash Fund 150.00
                            Cash 150.00

(2)   31   Automobile Expense 58.25
                          Miscellaneous Expense 33.18
                          Postage Expense 29.00
                          Supplies Expense 17.45
                          Telephone Expense 8.30
                          Cash Short and Over 2.70
                            Cash 148.88

Problem 2

Johnson Company
Bank Reconciliation
November 30, 200X

Bank statement balance, November 30		$12,735.00
Add:	$475.00	
	960.00	1,435.00
Subtotal		$14,170.00
Deduct: outstanding checks:		
No. 7246...	$ 99.45	
No. 7253...	512.50	
No. 7258...	183.00	794.95
Adjusted bank balance		$13,375.05
Ending check book balance, November 30		$ 8,506.05
Add: collection of note receivable	$5,000.00	
interest income	200.00	
error in recording check for office supplies	9.00	5,209.00
Subtotal		$13,715.05
Deduct: bank service charge	$ 15.00	
NSF check	325.00	
Adjusted check book balance...		$13,375.05

GENERAL JOURNAL   PAGE

DATE	DESCRIPTION	POST REF.	DEBIT	CREDIT
200X				
Nov. 30	Cash		5,200.00	
.	Note Receivable			5,000.00
	Interest Income			200.00
30	Cash		9.00	
	Office Supplies			9.00
30	Miscellaneous Expense		15.00	
	Cash			15.00
30	Accounts Receivable		325.00	
	Cash			325.00

CHAPTER 5 WORKING PAPERS
EXERCISE 5A-1

GENERAL JOURNAL

	DATE		DESCRIPTION	POST REF.	DEBIT	CREDIT	
1							1
2							2
3							3
4							4
5							5
6							6
7							7
8							8
9							9
10							10
11							11
12							12
13							13
14							14
15							15
16							16
17							17
18							18
19							19
20							20
21							21
22							22
23							23
24							24
25							25
26							26
27							27
28							28
29							29
30							30
31							31
32							32
33							33
34							34
35							35
36							36

EXERCISE 5A-2

GENERAL JOURNAL

	DATE		DESCRIPTION	POST REF.	DEBIT	CREDIT	
1							1
2							2
3							3
4							4
5							5
6							6
7							7
8							8
9							9
10							10
11							11
12							12
13							13
14							14
15							15
16							16
17							17
18							18
19							19
20							20
21							21
22							22
23							23
24							24
25							25
26							26
27							27
28							28
29							29
30							30
31							31
32							32
33							33
34							34
35							35
36							36

EXERCISE 5A-2—CONCLUDED

General Ledger
ACCOUNT Cash Short And Over   ACCOUNT NO. 585

DATE	ITEM	POST REF.	DEBIT	CREDIT	BALANCE	
					DEBIT	CREDIT

EXERCISE 5A-3

1. and 2.   **GENERAL JOURNAL**   PAGE 1

	DATE	DESCRIPTION	POST REF.	DEBIT	CREDIT	
1						1
2						2
3						3
4						4
5						5
6						6
7						7
8						8
9						9
10						10
11						11
12						12
13						13
14						14
15						15
16						16
17						17
18						18
19						19
20						20
21						21
22						22
23						23

EXERCISE 5A-4
1. and 2.
PETTY CASH PAYMENTS RECORD **FOR THE MONTH OF August, 200X** **PAGE 1**

DISTRIBUTION OF DEBITS

DAY	DESCRIPTION	VOU NO.	TOTAL AMOUNT	AUTO EXP	CHAR. CONTR. EXP	POST EXP.	TEL. EXP.	TRAV/ ENT. EXP.	MISC. EXP.	ACCOUNT	AMOUNT

Balance   _____

Replenished fund _____

Total   _____

PROBLEM 5A-5

1. and 2.

GENERAL JOURNAL

	DATE	DESCRIPTION	POST REF.	DEBIT	CREDIT	
1						1
2						2
3						3
4						4
5						5
6						6
7						7
8						8
9						9
10						10
11						11
12						12
13						13
14						14
15						15
16						16
17						17
18						18
19						19
20						20
21						21
22						22
23						23
24						24
25						25
26						26
27						27
28						28
29						29
30						30
31						31
32						32
33						33
34						34
35						35

PROBLEM 5A-5—CONCLUDED
3. and 4.

ACCOUNT Cash Short And Over   ACCOUNT NO. 585

DATE	ITEM	POST REF.	DEBIT	CREDIT	BALANCE	
					DEBIT	CREDIT

PROBLEM 5A-6
1. and 4.

GENERAL JOURNAL   PAGE 1

	DATE	DESCRIPTION	POST REF.	DEBIT	CREDIT	
1						1
2						2
3						3
4						4
5						5
6						6
7						7
8						8
9						9
10						10
11						11
12						12
13						13
14						14
15						15
16						16
17						17
18						18
19						19

PROBLEM 5A-6—CONCLUDED

2.–4.

PETTY CASH PAYMENTS RECORD   **FOR THE MONTH OF** __May 200X__   **PAGE**

DISTRIBUTION OF DEBITS

DAY	DESCRIPTION	VOU NO.	TOTAL AMOUNT	AUTO EXP.	CHAR. CONTR. EXP.	OFF. SUPP. EXP.	POST EXP.	TEL. EXP.	MISC. EXP.	ACCOUNT	AMOUNT

Balance   _____

Replenished fund   _____

Total   _____

PROBLEM 5A-7

1. and 2.

GENERAL JOURNAL

	DATE		DESCRIPTION	POST REF.	DEBIT	CREDIT	
1							1
2							2
3							3
4							4
5							5
6							6
7							7
8							8
9							9
10							10
11							11
12							12
13							13
14							14
15							15
16							16
17							17
18							18
19							19
20							20
21							21
22							22
23							23
24							24
25							25
26							26
27							27
28							28
29							29
30							30
31							31
32							32
33							33
34							34
35							35

PROBLEM 5A-7—CONCLUDED

3.

General Ledger
ACCOUNT Cash Short And Over   ACCOUNT NO. 585

DATE	ITEM	POST REF.	DEBIT	CREDIT	BALANCE	
					DEBIT	CREDIT

4.

PROBLEM 5A-8

1. and 4.

GENERAL JOURNAL

	DATE		DESCRIPTION	POST REF.	DEBIT	CREDIT	
1							1
2							2
3							3
4							4
5							5
6							6
7							7
8							8
9							9
10							10
11							11
12							12
13							13
14							14
15							15
16							16
17							17
18							18
19							19
20							20
21							21
22							22
23							23
24							24
25							25
26							26
27							27
28							28
29							29
30							30
31							31
32							32
33							33
34							34
35							35

PROBLEM 5A-8—CONCLUDED
2.–3.

PETTY CASH PAYMENTS RECORD   **FOR THE MONTH OF** ____June 200X____   **PAGE 1**

DISTRIBUTION OF DEBITS

DAY	DESCRIPTION	VOU NO.	TOTAL AMOUNT	AUTO EXP.	CHAR. CONTR. EXP.	OFF. SUPP. EXP.	POST EXP.	TEL. EXP.	MISC. EXP.	ACCOUNT	AMOUNT

Balance   _____

Replenished fund   _____

Total   _____

EXERCISE 5B-9

_____	1.	An endorsement where the depositor simply signs on the back of the check	a.	Signature card
_____	2.	An endorsement which contains words like "For Deposit Only" together with the signature	b.	Canceled check
_____	3.	A card filled out and signed by each person authorized to sign checks on an account	c.	Blank endorsement
_____	4.	The depositor who orders the bank to pay cash from the depositor's account	d.	Drawer
_____	5.	The bank on which the check is drawn	e.	Restrictive endorsement
_____	6.	The person being paid the cash	f.	Drawee
_____	7.	A check which has been paid by the bank and is being returned to the depositor	g.	Payee

EXERCISE 5B-10

Date   _____

Currency   _____

Coins   _____

Checks   _____

                   _____

                   _____

Total Deposit _____

EXERCISE 5B-11

NO. **40**						60-55 / 313
DATE _____ 20_____			**PAY**			NO. **40**
TO _____			**TO THE**		_____ 20_____	
FOR _____			**ORDER OF** _____		$ _____	
ACCT._____			_____ **DOLLARS**			
	DOLLARS	CENTS	FOR CLASSROOM USE ONLY			
BAL. BRO'T FOR'D						
AMT. DEPOSITED			PEOPLE'S BANK			
TOTAL			Wilkes-Barre, PA 18704-1455			
AMT. THIS CHECK				BY _____		
BAL. CAR'D FOR'D						

EXERCISE 5B-12

	Ending Bank Balance	Ending Checkbook Balance
a. Deposits in transit to the bank	_____	_____
b. Error in checkbook, check was recorded as $63 but was correctly written for $36	_____	_____
c. Debit memo for bank service charges	_____	_____
d. Outstanding checks	_____	_____
e. NSF check received from client	_____	_____
f. Error in bank deposit, appeared as $100 on the statement but was actually $1,000	_____	_____
g. Credit memo from bank advising they collected a note for us	_____	_____

EXERCISE 5B-13

GENERAL JOURNAL

PAGE 1

	DATE	DESCRIPTION	POST REF.	DEBIT	CREDIT	
1						1
2						2
3						3
4						4
5						5
6						6
7						7
8						8
9						9
10						10
11						11
12						12
13						13
14						14
15						15
16						16
17						17
18						18
19						19
20						20
21						21
22						22

PROBLEM 5B-14

1.

Linda Rogers Financial Consulting Service

Bank Reconciliation

July 31, 200X

Ending Bank Statement Balance

Add: _____   _____   _____

_____   _____   _____

Subtotal   _____

Deduct: _____   _____   _____

_____   _____   _____

_____   _____   _____

Adjusted Bank Statement Balance   _____

Ending Check Book Balance

Add: _____   _____

_____   _____

_____   _____

Subtotal   _____

Deduct: _____   _____

_____   _____

_____   _____

Adjusted Check Book Balance   _____

2.   **GENERAL JOURNAL**   PAGE 1

	DATE		DESCRIPTION	POST REF.	DEBIT	CREDIT	
1							1
2							2
3							3
4							4
5							5
6							6
7							7
8							8
9							9
10							10
11							11
12							12
13							13

PROBLEM 5B-15

1.

| Bank Reconciliation |
| November 30, 200X |

Ending Bank Statement Balance

Add: _____

_____

    Subtotal

Deduct: _____

_____

_____

Adjusted Bank Statement Balance

Ending Check Book Balance

Add: _____

_____

    Subtotal

Deduct: _____

_____

_____

Adjusted Check Book Balance

2.　　　　　　　　　　　　　**GENERAL JOURNAL**　　　　　　　　PAGE　1

	DATE	DESCRIPTION	POST REF.	DEBIT	CREDIT	
1						1
2						2
3						3
4						4
5						5
6						6
7						7
8						8
9						9
10						10
11						11
12						12
13						13

PROBLEM 5B-16

1.

Dennis Davis Athletic Foot Wear
Bank Reconciliation
May 20, 200X

Ending Bank Statement Balance _____

Add: _____ _____

_____ _____

  Subtotal _____

Deduct: _____ _____ _____

_____ _____ _____

_____ _____ _____

Adjusted Bank Statement Balance _____

Ending Check Book Balance

Add: _____ _____

_____ _____

_____ _____

  Subtotal _____

Deduct: _____ _____

_____ _____

_____ _____

Adjusted Check Book Balance _____

2.

GENERAL JOURNAL

PAGE 1

	DATE		DESCRIPTION	POST REF.	DEBIT	CREDIT	
1							1
2							2
3							3
4							4
5							5
6							6
7							7
8							8
9							9
10							10
11							11
12							12
13							13

PROBLEM 5B-17

1.

Bank Reconciliation

November 25, 200X

Ending Bank Statement Balance

Add: _____   _____   _____

_____   _____   _____

    Subtotal   _____

Deduct: _____   _____   _____

_____   _____   _____

_____   _____   _____

Adjusted Bank Statement Balance   _____

Ending Check Book Balance

Add: _____   _____

_____   _____

_____   _____

    Subtotal   _____

Deduct: _____   _____

_____   _____

_____   _____

Adjusted Check Book Balance   _____

2.   **GENERAL JOURNAL**   PAGE 1

	DATE	DESCRIPTION	POST REF.	DEBIT	CREDIT	
1						1
2						2
3						3
4						4
5						5
6						6
7						7
8						8
9						9
10						10
11						11
12						12
13						13

CHALLENGE PROBLEM

GENERAL JOURNAL

	DATE		DESCRIPTION	POST REF.	DEBIT	CREDIT	
1							1
2							2
3							3
4							4
5							5
6							6
7							7
8							8
9							9
10							10
11							11
12							12
13							13
14							14
15							15
16							16
17							17
18							18
19							19
20							20
21							21
22							22
23							23
24							24
25							25
26							26
27							27
28							28
29							29
30							30
31							31
32							32
33							33
34							34
35							35
36							36

CHALLENGE PROBLEM

GENERAL JOURNAL

PAGE 2

	DATE	DESCRIPTION	POST REF.	DEBIT	CREDIT	
1						1
2						2
3						3
4						4
5						5
6						6
7						7
8						8
9						9
10						10
11						11
12						12
13						13
14						14
15						15
16						16
17						17
18						18
19						19
20						20
21						21
22						22
23						23
24						24
25						25
26						26
27						27
28						28
29						29
30						30
31						31
32						32
33						33
34						34
35						35
36						36

CHAPTER 6

PAYROLL ACCOUNTING

PRACTICE TEST

Part I—True/False

Please circle the correct answer.

T F 1. A monthly salary is paid to independent contractors, subject to withholdings and payroll taxes.

T F 2. Income tax withholdings from paychecks of employees are based on the withholding allowances claim on Form W-4.

T F 3. The Fair Labor Standards Act requires that employers pay one and one-half times the regular rate for overtime wages.

T F 4. Social security and Medicare tax rates are fixed and withholding amounts are computed only once for several years at a time.

T F 5. To record the payroll, Salary or Wage Expense is debited for the total gross earnings.

T F 6. Employees Income Tax Payable is the liability account where social security taxes deducted from employees would be recorded.

T F 7. Gross pay or wages would include regular pay, overtime pay, and any other premium pay earned during the period.

T F 8. Employee Charitable Contributions Payable represents an optional deduction from employees' wages.

T F 9. Social security taxes and income tax withholdings are remitted by the employer to the appropriate government agency.

T F 10. To journalize the employer's payroll taxes, the account Wage or Salary Expense is debited for the total amount of tax levied.

Part II—Multiple Choice

Please circle the correct answer.

1. Employee's Income Tax Payable is a liability account used to record
    a. Social security taxes withheld
    b. Federal income taxes withheld
    c. Medicare taxes withheld
    d. Unemployment taxes withheld

2. The difference between gross wages and withholdings (required and optional) is called
    a. Employer's tax liability
    b. Payroll taxes
    c. Wages or salary payable
    d. Gross earnings

3. Which of these taxes is matched by the employer for amounts withheld from employees' paychecks?
    a. Social security taxes
    b. Unemployment taxes
    c. All required withholdings
    d. All optional withholdings

4. Which of these is levied only against the employer?
    a. Social security taxes
    b. Unemployment taxes
    c. Income taxes
    d. Health insurance premiums

5. To record the employer's payroll taxes, which account is debited?
    a. Payroll Expense
    b. Payroll Tax Expense
    c. Income Taxes Payable
    d. Wages or Salary Expense

6. If a person's regular hourly rate is $6.50 an hour, what is his or her overtime rate?
    a. $13.00 per hour
    b. $8.00 per hour
    c. $9.75 per hour
    d. $3.25 per hour

7. Which of these is an optional deduction?
    a. Social security taxes
    b. Income taxes
    c. State and local taxes
    d. Health insurance premiums

8. What determines how much an employer will withhold from an employee's paycheck for income taxes?
    a. Base pay
    b. Minimum wage laws
    c. Withholding allowances claimed
    d. Tax brackets

9. A multi-column form used to collect and compute payroll data for all employees is called a(n)
    a. Payroll Register
    b. Employee Earnings Record
    c. General Journal
    d. General Ledger Account

10. To record the payroll, which of the following accounts is debited?
    a. Payroll Tax Expense
    b. Wages Payable
    c. Employee Income Taxes Payable
    d. Wage or Salary Expense

Part III—Fill in the Blank

1. When the regular rate is multiplied times one and a half, the result is called the _____ rate.

2. Social security taxes levied for purposes of retirement are known by the abbreviation, _____ taxes.

3. Social security taxes levied for health insurance (Medicare) are known by the abbreviation, _____ taxes.

4. When gross earnings, deductions, and net pay of employees is recorded, it is called _____.

5. Employers' payroll taxes include matching _____, federal unemployment taxes, and state unemployment taxes.

6. A monthly _____ is paid to workers who receive regular and equal paychecks for services performed.

7. An employee may claim a(n) _____ for himself or herself, plus additional amounts if tax deductions will justify it.

8. A(n) _____ is used to record earnings and deductions for all employees.

9. A payroll tax collected to finance the cost of federal unemployment programs is called _____.

10. All states have unemployment compensation laws which provide for a payroll tax called _____.

Part IV—Practice Problems

Practice Problem 1—Computing Gross Pay

Required:

Based on the information provided, compute gross wages for the following people:

a. James Richardson worked 44 hours last week. His regular rate of pay is $9.20 per hour.
b. Janice Williams worked 48 hours last week. Her regular rate of pay is $12.50 per hour.
c. Dan Ferguson worked 42 hours last week. His regular rate of pay is $8.40 per hour.
d. Maile Baures's annual salary is $24,800. What is her weekly pay?

(a)_____

(b)_____

(c)_____

(d)_____

Practice Problem 2—Recording the Payroll and Employer's Payroll Taxes

Crannell Company had the following payroll information:

Gross wages: $5,860
     OASDI taxes withheld: $379.60
     HI taxes withheld: $87.90
     Federal income taxes withheld: $840
     Health insurance premiums withheld: $400

Required:

    a. Prepare the journal entry to record the payroll.
    b. Assuming that all wages are subject to both FUTA and SUTA and the rates are .8% and 5.4% respectively, record the employer's payroll taxes.

GENERAL JOURNAL

PAGE

	DATE	DESCRIPTION	POST REF.	DEBIT	CREDIT	
1						1
2						2
3						3
4						4
5						5
6						6
7						7
8						8
9						9
10						10
11						11
12						12
13						13
14						14
15						15
16						16
17						17
18						18
19						19
20						20
21						21
22						22
23						23
24						24
25						25

SOLUTIONS TO PRACTICE TEST

Part I	Part II	Part III
1. F	1. b	1. overtime
2. T	2. c	2. OASDI
3. T	3. a	3. HI
4. F	4. b	4. recording the payroll
5. T	5. b	5. social security and medicare taxes
6. F	6. c	6. salary
7. T	7. d	7. withholding allowance
8. T	8. c	8. payroll register
9. T	9. a	9. FUTA
10. F	10. d	10. SUTA

Part IV

Practice Problem 1

a. 40 ×   9.20 = $368.00
     4 × 13.80 =   55.20
                       $423.20

b. 40 × 12.50 = $500.00
     8 × 18.75 =   150.00
                       $650.00

c. 40 ×   8.40 = $336.00
     2 × 12.60 =   25.20
                       $361.20

d. $24,800 ÷ 52 = $476.92

Practice Problem 2

a. To record the payroll:

Payroll Expense	5,860.00	
FICA—OASDI Tax Payable		379.60
FICA—HI Tax Payable		87.90
Employees Income Taxes Payable		840.00
Health Insurance Payable		400.00
Wages Payable		4,152.50
Payroll for January 18		

b. To record the employer's payroll taxes:

Payroll Tax Expense	830.82	
FICA—OASDI Tax Payable		379.60
FICA—HI Tax Payable		87.90
FUTA Tax Payable		46.88
SUTA Tax Payable		316.44

CHAPTER 6 WORKING PAPERS

EXERCISE 6A-1

a.

b.

c.

d.

EXERCISE 6A-2

a.

b.

c.

d.

EXERCISE 6A-3

a.

b.

c.

d.

This page not used.

PROBLEM 6A-4

Payroll Register (Continues on facing page)

Name	Emp. No.	# of Allw.	M/S	Earnings			
				Regular	Overtime	Total	Cum. Total

PROBLEM 6A-5
Employee Earnings Record

Name: _____   Sex: _____
Address: _____   Marital Status: _____
City: _____   Allowances: _____

Earnings			[7,000] Unemploy. Comp.	[90,000] FICA— OASDI	Tax 6.5%	FICA–HI	Taxable Earnings Tax 1.5%
Regular	Overtime	Total					

PROBLEM 6A-4—CONCLUDED

Payroll Register (Continued from facing page)

Earnings and Deductions

FICA—OASDI	Tax 6.5%	FICA—HI	Tax 1.5%	Federal Inc. Tax	Health Insurance	Credit Union (Savings)	Pension	Total Deductions	Net Paycheck	Check #

PROBLEM 6A-5--CONCLUDED

Employee Earnings Record (Continued from facing page)

Department: _____   Social Security Number: _____
Occupation: _____   Date of Birth: _____
Pay Rate: _____   Date Employed: _____

and Deductions

Federal Inc. Tax	Health Insurance	Credit Union	Other	Total	Net Paycheck	Week

PROBLEM 6A-6

GENERAL JOURNAL   PAGE

	DATE		DESCRIPTION	POST REF.	DEBIT	CREDIT	
1							1
2							2
3							3
4							4
5							5
6							6
7							7
8							8
9							9
10							10
11							11
12							12
13							13
14							14
15							15
16							16
17							17
18							18
19							19
20							20
21							21
22							22
23							23
24							24
25							25
26							26
27							27
28							28
29							29
30							30
31							31
32							32
33							33
34							34
35							35

This page not used.

PROBLEM 6A-7

Payroll Register (Continues on facing page)

Name	Emp. No.	# of Allw.	M/S	Earnings			
				Regular	Overtime	Total	Cum. Total

PROBLEM 6A-8

Employee Earnings Record

Name: _____   Sex: _____

Address: _____   Marital Status: _____

City: _____   Allowances: _____

Earnings							Taxable Earnings
Regular	Overtime	Total	[7,000] Unemploy. Comp.	[90,000] FICA— OASDI	Tax 6.5%	FICA–HI	Tax 1.5%

PROBLEM 6A-7—CONCLUDED

Payroll Register (Continued from facing page)

Earnings and Deductions

FICA— OASDI	Tax 6.5%	FICA—HI	Tax 1.5%	Federal Inc. Tax	Health Insurance	(Savings) Credit Union	Other (Charity)	Total Deductions	Net Paycheck	Check #

PROBLEM 6A-8—CONCLUDED

Employee Earnings Record (Continued from facing page)

Department: _____   Social Security Number: _____
Occupation: _____   Date of Birth: _____
Pay Rate: _____   Date Employed: _____

and Deductions

Federal Inc. Tax	Health Insurance	Credit Union	Other	Total	Net Paycheck	Week

PROBLEM 6A-9

GENERAL JOURNAL   PAGE

	DATE		DESCRIPTION	POST REF.	DEBIT	CREDIT	
1							1
2							2
3							3
4							4
5							5
6							6
7							7
8							8
9							9
10							10
11							11
12							12
13							13
14							14
15							15
16							16
17							17
18							18
19							19
20							20
21							21

EXERCISE 6B-10

a.

b.

EXERCISE 6B-11

| | FICA TAXES | | | |
	OASDI	HI	FUTA TAX PAYABLE	SUTA TAX PAYABLE
Matt Kingston				
Kyra Billings				
Jessica Clark				
Ella Gazabara				

EXERCISE 6B-12
a. and b.

GENERAL JOURNAL   PAGE

	DATE	DESCRIPTION	POST REF.	DEBIT	CREDIT	
1						1
2						2
3						3
4						4
5						5
6						6
7						7
8						8
9						9
10						10
11						11
12						12
13						13
14						14
15						15
16						16
17						17
18						18
19						19

PROBLEM 6B-13

EMPLOYEE	GROSS EARNINGS	DEDUCTIONS FEDERAL TAX	FICA	HI	TOTAL	NET PAY	FUTA TAX	SUTA TAX
Connie Bruchman								
Alexa Dorokhova								
Richard Owens								
Kyle Peterson								
Totals								

PROBLEM 6B-14

a.–d.   GENERAL JOURNAL   PAGE _____

	DATE		DESCRIPTION	POST REF.	DEBIT	CREDIT	
1							1
2							2
3							3
4							4
5							5
6							6
7							7
8							8
9							9
10							10
11							11
12							12
13							13
14							14
15							15
16							16
17							27
18							18
19							19
20							20
21							21
22							22
23							23
24							24
25							25
26							26
27							27
28							28
29							29
30							30
31							31
32							32
33							33
34							34
35							35
36							36

PROBLEM 6B-15
a.–d.

GENERAL JOURNAL PAGE

	DATE		DESCRIPTION	POST REF.	DEBIT	CREDIT	
1							1
2							2
3							3
4							4
5							5
6							6
7							7
8							8
9							9
10							10
11							11
12							12
13							13
14							14
15							15
16							16
17							27
18							18
19							19
20							20
21							21
22							22
23							23
24							24
25							25
26							26
27							27
28							28
29							29
30							30
31							31
32							32
33							33
34							34
35							35

PROBLEM 6B-16

EMPLOYEE	GROSS EARN.	DEDUCTIONS			TOTAL	NET PAY	FUTA TAX	SUTA TAX
		FED. TAX	FICA	HI				
Alice Burns								
Mark Clooney								
Raoul Matthews								
Darbi Pearson								
Totals								

PROBLEM 6B-17

a.–d. **GENERAL JOURNAL** PAGE 1

	DATE	DESCRIPTION	POST REF.	DEBIT	CREDIT	
1						1
2						2
3						3
4						4
5						5
6						6
7						7
8						8
9						9
10						10
11						11
12						12
13						13
14						14
15						15
16						16
17						27
18						18
19						19
20						20
21						21
22						22
23						23
24						24
25						25
26						26
27						27
28						28
29						29

PROBLEM 6B-17—CONCLUDED

a.–d.   **GENERAL JOURNAL**   PAGE 2

	DATE	DESCRIPTION	POST REF.	DEBIT	CREDIT	
1						1
2						2
3						3
4						4
5						5
6						6
7						7
8						8
9						9
10						10
11						11
12						12
13						13
14						14
15						15

PROBLEM 6B-18

a.–d.   **GENERAL JOURNAL**   PAGE 1

	DATE	DESCRIPTION	POST REF.	DEBIT	CREDIT	
1						1
2						2
3						3
4						4
5						5
6						6
7						7
8						8
9						9
10						10
11						11
12						12
13						13
14						14
15						15
16						16

PROBLEM 6B-18—CONCLUDED

a.–d.   **GENERAL JOURNAL**   PAGE 2

	DATE		DESCRIPTION	POST REF.	DEBIT	CREDIT	
1							1
2							2
3							3
4							4
5							5
6							6
7							7
8							8
9							9
10							10
11							11
12							12
13							13
14							14
15							15
16							16
17							27
18							18
19							19
20							20
21							21
22							22
23							23
24							24
25							25
26							26
27							27
28							28
29							29
30							30
31							31
32							32
33							33
34							34
35							35
36							36

CHALLENGE PROBLEM

1.

EMPLOYEE	GROSS EARN.	DEDUCTIONS			HEALTH INS.	TOTAL	NET PAY	FUTA TAX	SUTA TAX
		FEDERAL TAX	FICA— OASDI	FICA— HI					
Art Krekow									
E. Washington									
M. Francisco									
James Klein									
Totals									

2.   **GENERAL JOURNAL**   PAGE   1

	DATE	DESCRIPTION	POST REF.	DEBIT	CREDIT	
1						1
2						2
3						3
4						4
5						5
6						6
7						7
8						8
9						9
10						10
11						11
12						12
13						13
14						14
15						15
16						16
17						27
18						18
19						19
20						20
21						21
22						22
23						23
24						24
28						28
29						29

CHALLENGE PROBLEM—CONCLUDED

3.   **GENERAL JOURNAL**   PAGE 2

	DATE	DESCRIPTION	POST REF.	DEBIT	CREDIT	
1						1
2						2
3						3
4						4
5						5
6						6
7						7
8						8
9						9
10						10
11						11
12						12

4.   **GENERAL JOURNAL**   PAGE 3

	DATE	DESCRIPTION	POST REF.	DEBIT	CREDIT	
1						1
2						2
3						3
4						4
5						5
6						6
7						7
8						8
9						9
10						10
11						11
12						12
13						13
14						14
15						15
16						16
17						17
18						18
19						19
20						20

CHAPTER 7

ACCOUNTING FOR ATTORNEYS

PRACTICE TEST

Part I—True/False

Please circle the correct answer.

T F 1. Under the accrual basis of accounting, revenue and expenses are recognized when earned or incurred, regardless of when cash is received.

T F 2. Under the accrual basis of accounting, a sale made on account involves a credit to revenue and a debit to cash.

T F 3. Under the accrual basis of accounting, a bill received today but paid later involves a debit to an expense account and a credit to accounts payable.

T F 4. A person or company being sued is called the plaintiff.

T F 5. A lawyer's office docket is a form used to maintain a memorandum record of each legal case with a client.

T F 6. A lawyer's collection docket is a form used to maintain a record of amounts collected from the debtor and the amounts paid to the creditor.

T F 7. Funds received or collected by an attorney and held for a client must be deposited in a separate bank account after deducting the attorney's collection fee.

T F 8. The account "Advances on Behalf of Clients" is used by an attorney when paying such items as court filing fees, fees charged by accountants for doing audits, and the cost of obtaining depositions made on behalf of the client.

T F 9. Funds received or collected by an attorney are debited to "Clients' Trust Account" and credited to "Collection Fees Revenue."

T F 10. When an amount collected by an attorney is later paid to the client, the account "Client's Trust Account" is debited and "Liability for Trust Funds" is credited.

Part II—Multiple Choice

Please circle the correct answer.

1. The basis of accounting that recognizes revenue and expenses when earned or incurred, regardless of when cash is received or paid, is called the
    a. Accrual basis
    b. Cash basis
    c. Modified cash basis
    d. All the above

Part II—Continued

2. The basis of accounting that recognizes revenue and expenses only when cash is received or paid is called the
   a. Accrual basis
   b. Cash basis
   c. Accounting basis
   d. Revenue and expense basis

3. Funds received or collected by an attorney and held for a client are debited to "Clients' Trust Account," and credited to
   a. Liability for Trust Funds
   b. Collection Fees Revenue
   c. Advances on Behalf of Clients
   d. Legal Fees Revenue

4. A person or company bringing a suit against someone else is called the
   a. Defendant
   b. Plaintiff
   c. Docket
   d. Creditor

5. The person or company being sued is called the
   a. Creditor
   b. Debtor
   c. Defendant
   d. Plaintiff

6. An attorney collected a $1,000 debt, on a 25% commission basis, for a client. The proper journal entry would include a
   a. Debit to Cash for $750
   b. Debit to Clients' Trust Account for $250
   c. Credit to Liability for Trust Funds for $750
   d. Credit to Collection Fees Revenue for $750

7. An attorney collected a $1,000 debit on a 25% commission basis for a client. When the amount collected is paid to the client, the proper journal entry would include a
   a. Debit to Liability for Trust Funds for $750
   b. Credit to Liability for Trust Funds for $250
   c. Debit to Clients' Trust Account for $750
   d. Credit to Clients' Trust Account for $250

8. When an attorney makes payments for items such as court filing fees, fees charged by accountants for doing audits, and the cost of obtaining depositions made on behalf of clients, the proper journal entry would include a
   a. Debit to Miscellaneous Expense
   b. Credit to Liability for Trust Funds
   c. Credit to Clients' Trust Account
   d. Debit to Advances on Behalf of Clients

Part II—Concluded

9. A form used by an attorney to maintain a memorandum record of each legal case with a client is called a(n)
   a. Accounts Receivable Ledger
   b. Accounts Payable Ledger
   c. Office Docket
   d. Memorandum File

10. When an attorney is hired to collect an outstanding debt, the form used to maintain a record of cash collections from the debtor and cash payments to the client, is called a(n)
    a. Accounts Payable Ledger
    b. Collection Docket
    c. Accounts Receivable Ledger
    d. Debtor File

Part III—Fill in the Blank

1. The _____ basis of accounting recognizes revenue and expenses when earned or incurred, regardless of when cash is received.

2. The basis of accounting that recognizes revenue and expenses only when cash is received or paid, with no adjustments for depreciation of long-term assets or for the usage of supplies and other prepaid assets, is called the _____ basis.

3. The basis of accounting that recognizes revenue and expenses only when cash is received or paid, but allows for year-end adjustments for depreciation of long-term assets or for the usage of supplies and other prepaid assets, is called the _____ basis.

4. A person or company bringing a suit against someone else is called the _____.

5. A person or company being sued is called the _____.

6. Funds received or collected by an attorney and held for a client must be deposited in a separate bank account, after deducting the attorney's collection fee. The account debited is called the _____, and the account credited is called the _____.

7. An attorney received a check for $40,000, representing the balance due for legal fees of $3,200 and for an $800 payment for work done by an accountant and paid by the attorney. The attorney debited Advances on Behalf of Clients for $800 when the payment was made. The proper journal entry by the attorney to record the receipt of $4,000 would be a debit to _____ for $4,000 and credit to _____ for $3,200 and a credit to _____ for $800.

8. A(n) _____ is a form used to maintain a memorandum record of each legal case with a client.

9. Lawyers who collect accounts for clients may use a form known as a _____.

10. The _____ is a book of original entry to record all payments of cash.

Part IV—Practice Problems

Practice Problem 1—Lawyer's Collection Docket

Darlene Robertson, an attorney, has been engaged to collect a debt owed by Cindy Rowland, Cascade Athletic Club. Vicker's collection docket is reproduced below.

Debtor—Cindy Rowland
Address—9109 East Burnside, City
Creditor—Cascade Athletic Club
Address—278 Division Street
Date claim received—4/16/0X
No. 845
Date disposed of—6/11/0X
Total amount—$1,200
Amount collected—$1,200
Fee—$400
Amount remitted—$800
Check No.—60, 66, 75

Received from creditor

DATE	FOR	AMOUNT
4/30	Fee	$200.00
5/16	Fee	$100.00
6/5	Fee	$100.00

Received from debtor

DATE	AMOUNT
4/30	$600.00
5/16	$300.00
6/5	$300.00

Paid to creditor

DATE	CHECK NO.	AMOUNT
5/7	60	$400.00
5/23	66	$200.00
6/11	75	$200.00

Remarks: Statement of account. Collection fee 33 1/3%. No suit without further instruction.

Required:

Enter the information above in the collection docket.

Practice Problem 1—Concluded

Collection Docket

Debtor		Date claim rec'd		No.
Address		Date Disposed of		
		Total Amount		
Business		Amount Collected		
Creditor		Fee		
Address		Expense		
		Amount Remitted		
Rec'd claim from		Check No.		
Attorney for debtor		**Received from Creditor**		
Calls on debtor		Date	For	Amount
Correspondence				

Received from Debtor				Paid to Creditor			
Date	Amount	Date	Amount	Check No.	Amount	Check No.	Amount

Remarks

Practice Problem 2—Special Journal Entries

Dude Kennedy is an attorney engaged in the practice of law. A partial chart of accounts and selected transactions for March of the current year are listed below.

DUDE KENNEDY, ATTORNEY AT LAW
Partial Chart Of Accounts

ASSETS
  111 Cash
  121 Clients' Trust Account
  131 Advances on Behalf of Clients
LIABILITIES
  221 Liability for Trust Funds
  231 Employees' Income Tax Payable
  232 FICA Tax Payable—OASDI
  241 FUTA Tax Payable
  251 SUTA Tax Payable

OWNER'S EQUITY
  312 Dude Kennedy, Drawing
REVENUE
  411 Legal Fees
  421 Collection Fees
EXPENSES
  542 Salary Expense
  552 Payroll Taxes Expense

Mar. 5 Received a check for $1,500 from Steve Fielder in payment of the amount due on Collection No. 33. Kennedy had agreed to handle this collection for the Quality Appliance Store on a 33 1/3% commission basis.

9 Paid $900 to Sharla Knox, an accountant, for work on case no. 67. check no. 220.

12 Received a check for $525 from Womack and Sons, architects, for drafting a partnership agreement.

15 Paid semimonthly salary to Sheryl Hansen, secretary, in the amount of $950, less income tax, $123, less FICA Tax Payable—OASDI $58.90, less FICA Tax Payable—HI $13.78. Issued check no. 221 for $754.32.

15 Kennedy withdrew $2,000 for personal use. Check no. 222.

15 Paid employee's income tax, $246, FICA Tax Payable—OASDI $235.60, and FICA Tax Payable—HI $55.12 on last month's wages to the Oregon National Bank. Issued check No. 223 for $536.72

22 Issued Check No. 44 in the amount of $1,000 to the Quality Appliance Store. Collection No. 33.

26 Received a check for $1,800 from Jasper Corporation in full payment of case no. 67. This remittance is in payment of the balance due for legal fees, $1,500, and $300 for payment of the accountant's fee paid by Kennedy on March 5 and debited to Advances on Behalf of Clients.

27 Received a check for $635 from Deborah Mueller for preparing a will.

31 Paid semimonthly salary to Sheryl Hansen, secretary, in the amount of $950, less income tax, $123, less FICA Tax Payable—OASDI $58.90, less FICA Tax Payable—HI $13.78. Issued check no. 224 for $754.32.

31 Kennedy withdrew $2,000 for personal use. Check no. 225.

Required:

1. Record the foregoing transactions in the cash receipts journal and the cash payments journal reproduced on the following pages.
2. Foot and prove the totals.

PRACTICE PROBLEM 2—CONCLUDED

CASH RECEIPTS JOURNAL   Page   1

DATE	DESCRIPTION	POST REF.	GENERAL CR.	REVENUE		LIAB. FOR TRUST FUNDS 221 CR.	CLIENTS TRUST ACCT. 121 DR.	CASH 111 DR.
				Legal Fees 411 CR.	Coll. Fees 421 CR.			

Total debits   _____

Total credits   _____

CASH PAYMENTS JOURNAL   Page   1

DATE	DESCRIPTION	POST REF.	GENERAL DR.	LIAB. FOR TRUST FUNDS 221 CR.	SALARY EXP. 542 DR.	EMP. INC. TAX PAY. 231 CR.	FICA TAX PAY OASDI 232 CR.	FICA TAX PAY HI 233 CR.	CHECK NO.	CLIENT'S TRUST ACCT. 121 CR.	CHECK NO.	CASH 111 CR.

Total debits   _____

Total credits   _____

SOLUTIONS TO PRACTICE TEST

Part I	Part II	Part III
1. T	1. a	1. accrual
2. F	2. b	2. cash
3. T	3. a	3. modified cash
4. F	4. b	4. plantiff
5. T	5. c	5. defendant
6. T	6. c	6. Clients' Trust Account; Liability for Trust Funds
7. T	7. a	7. Cash, Legal Fees Revenue; Advances on Behalf of Clients
8. T	8. d	8. Office Docket
9. F	9. c	9. Collective Docket
10. F	10. b	10. Cash Payments Journal

Part IV
Practice Problem 1
EXERCISE 7-4
Collection Docket

Debtor		Date claim rec'd	4-16-0X			No. 845		
	Cindy Rowland	Date Disposed of		6-11-0X				
Address	9109 East Burnside, City	Total Amount		$1,200				
		Amount Collected		$1,200				
Business		Fee		$400				
Creditor	Cascade Athletic Club	Expense						
Address	278 Division Street, City	Amount Remitted		$800				
		Check No.		60, 66, 75				
Rec'd claim from		**Received from Creditor**						
Attorney for debtor		Date	For			Amount		
Calls on debtor		4/30	Fee		2	0	0	00
Correspondence		5/16	Fee		1	0	0	00
		6/5	Fee		1	0	0	00

Received from Debtor						Paid to Creditor									
Date		Amount				Date	Amount				Check No.	Amount				Check No.	Amount
4	30	6	0	0	00							60	4	0	0	00		
5	16	3	0	0	00							66	2	0	0	00		
6	5	3	0	0	00							75	2	0	0	00		

Remarks   Statement of account. Collection fee 33 1/3%

No suit without further instructions.

Practice Problem 2

CASH RECEIPTS JOURNAL   Page   1

DATE		DESCRIPTION	POST REF.	GENERAL CR.	REVENUE		LIAB. FOR TRUST FUNDS 221 CR.	CLIENTS TRUST ACCT. 121 DR.	CASH 111 DR.
					Legal Fees 411 CR.	Coll. Fees 421 CR.			
200X Mar.	5	Steve Fielder, Collection No. 33				500.00	1,000.00	1,000.00	500.00
	12	Womack and Sons—Partnership							
		Agreement			525.00				525.00
	26	Advances on Behalf of Clients—							
		Case No. 67		300.00	1,500.00				1,800.00
	27	Deborah Mueller—Will			635.00				635.00
				300.00	2,660.00	500.00	1,000.00	1,000.00	3,460.00

Total debits   4,460.00

Total credits   4,460.00

CASH PAYMENTS JOURNAL   Page   1

DATE		DESCRIPTION	POST REF.	GENERAL DR.	LIAB. FOR TRUST FUNDS 221 CR.	SALARY EXP. 542 DR.	EMP. INC. TAX PAY. 231 CR.	FICA TAX PAY OASDI 232 CR.	FICA TAX PAY HI 233 CR.	CHECK NO.	CLIENT'S TRUST ACCT. 121 CR.	CHECK NO.	CASH 111 CR.
200X Mar.	9	Advances on Behalf of											
		Clients		900.00								220	900.00
	15	Sheryl Hansen				950.00	123.00	58.90	13.78			221	754.32
	15	Dude Kennedy, Drawing		2,000.00								222	2,000.00
	15	Employees' Income Tax Pay.		246.00									
		FICA Tax Payable—OASDI		235.60									
		FICA Tax Payable—HI		55.12								223	536.72
	22	Collection No. 33			1,000.00					44	1,000.00		
	31	Sheryl Hansen				950.00	123.00	58.90	13.78			224	754.32
	31	Dude Kennedy, Drawing		2,000.00								225	2,000.00
				5,436.72	1,000.00	1,900.00	246.00	117.80	27.56		1,000.00		6,945.36

Total debits   8,336.72

Total credits   8,336.72

CHAPTER 7 WORKING PAPERS

EXERCISE 7-1

_____	1.	Accrual basis	a. The person or company being sued
			b. An auxiliary record which provides a complete record of each legal case
_____	2.	Cash basis	c. Revenues and expenses are recognized when earned or occurred, regardless of when cash is received.
_____	3.	Collection docket	d. An auxiliary record which provides a record of the amounts collected from the debtor and the amounts paid to the creditor
_____	4.	Defendant	e. Revenues and expenses are recognized only when cash is received or paid.
			f. A person or company bringing a suit against someone else.
_____	5.	Office docket	
_____	6.	Plaintiff	

EXERCISE 7-2

EXERCISE 7-2

Client

Address   No.

IN RE:

Court

Court File No.   20

Calendar No.   Attorney for

Other Attorneys

Nature of Matter

Remarks

Services Rendered

Fees and Payments

Moneys Received

Purpose

Amount

Balance Due

Date

Carried Forward

EXERCISE 7-3

CASH RECEIPTS JOURNAL   Page   1

DATE	DESCRIPTION	POST REF.	GENERAL CR.	REVENUE Legal Fees 411 CR.	REVENUE Coll. Fees 421 CR.	LIAB. FOR TRUST FUNDS 221 CR.	CLIENTS TRUST ACCT. 121 DR.	CASH 111 DR.
20xx								

Total debits   _____

Total credits   _____

CASH PAYMENTS JOURNAL   Page   1

DATE	DESCRIPTION	POST REF.	GENERAL DR.	LIAB. FOR TRUST FUNDS 221 DR.	SALARY EXP. 542 DR.	EMP. INC. TAX PAY. 231 CR.	FICA TAX PAY OASDI 232 CR.	FICA TAX PAY. HI 233 CR.	CHECK NO.	CLIENT'S TRUST ACCT. 121 CR.	CHECK NO.	CASH 111 CR

Total debits   _____

Total credits   _____

EXERCISE 7-4

Collection Docket

Debtor		Date claim rec'd		No.		
Address		Date Disposed of				
		Total Amount				
Business		Amount Collected				
Creditor		Fee				
Address		Expense				
		Amount Remitted				
Rec'd claim from		Check No.				
Attorney for debtor		**Received from Creditor**				
Calls on debtor		Date	For	Amount		
Correspondence						

Received from Debtor				**Paid to Creditor**			
Date	Amount	Date	Amount	Check No.	Amount	Check No.	Amount

Remarks

EXERCISE 7-5

CASH RECEIPTS JOURNAL   Page 1

DATE	DESCRIPTION	POST REF.	GENERAL CR.	REVENUE Legal Fees 411 CR.	Coll. Fees 421 CR.	LIAB. FOR TRUST FUNDS 221 CR.	CLIENTS TRUST ACCT. 121 DR.	CASH 111 DR.

Total debits _____

Total credits _____

CASH PAYMENTS JOURNAL   Page 1

DATE	DESCRIPTION	POST REF.	GENERAL DR.	LIAB. FOR TRUST FUNDS 221 DR.	SALARY EXP. 542 DR.	EMP. INC. TAX PAY. 231 CR.	FICA TAX PAY OASDI 232 CR.	FICA TAX PAY HI 233 CR.	CHECK NO.	CLIENT'S TRUST ACCT. 121 CR.	CHECK NO.	CASH 111 CR.

Total debits _____

Total credits _____

PROBLEM 7-6
1.—3.

CASH RECEIPTS JOURNAL   Page 1

DATE	DESCRIPTION	POST REF.	GENERAL CR.	Legal Fees 411 CR.	Coll. Fees 421 CR.	LIAB. FOR TRUST FUNDS 221 CR.	CLIENTS TRUST ACCT. 121 DR.	CASH 111 DR.

Total debits _____

Total credits _____

CASH PAYMENTS JOURNAL   Page 1

DATE	DESCRIPTION	POST REF.	GENERAL DR.	LIAB. FOR TRUST FUNDS 221 DR.	SALARY EXP. 542 DR.	EMP. INC. TAX PAY. 231 CR.	FICA TAX PAY OASDI 232 CR.	FICA TAX PAY HI 233 CR.	CHECK NO.	CLIENT'S TRUST ACCT. 121 CR.	CHECK NO.	CASH 111 CR.

Total debits _____

Total credits _____

PROBLEM 7-6—CONTINUED

1.
GENERAL JOURNAL

PAGE   1

	DATE		DESCRIPTION	POST REF.	DEBIT	CREDIT	
1							1
2							2
3							3
4							4
5							5
6							6
7							7
8							8
9							9
10							10
11							11
12							12
13							13
14							14
15							15
16							16
17							17
18							18
19							19
20							20
21							21
22							22
23							23
24							24
25							25
26							26
27							27
28							28
29							29
30							30
31							31
32							32
33							33
34							34
35							35
36							36

PROBLEM 7-6—CONCLUDED
2. and 3.

PROBLEM 7-7
1.—3.

CASH RECEIPTS JOURNAL   Page

DATE	DESCRIPTION	POST REF.	GENERAL CR.	REVENUE Legal Fees 411 CR.	Coll. Fees 421 CR.	LIAB. FOR TRUST FUNDS 221 CR.	CLIENTS TRUST ACCT. 121 DR.	CASH 111 DR.

Total debits _____

Total credits _____

CASH PAYMENTS JOURNAL   Page

DATE	DESCRIPTION	POST REF.	GENERAL DR.	LIAB. FOR TRUST FUNDS 221 DR.	SALARY EXP. 542 DR.	EMP. INC. TAX PAY. 231 CR.	FICA TAX PAY OASDI 232 CR.	FICA TAX PAY HI 233 CR.	CHECK NO.	CLIENT'S TRUST ACCT. 121 CR.	CHECK NO.	CASH 111 CR.

Total debits _____

Total credits _____

PROBLEM 7-7—CONTINUED

1. and 3.   **GENERAL JOURNAL**   PAGE 1

	DATE		DESCRIPTION	POST REF.	DEBIT	CREDIT	
1							1
2							2
3							3
4							4
5							5
6							6
7							7
8							8
9							9
10							10
11							11
12							12
13							13
14							14
15							15
16							16
17							17
18							18
19							19
20							20
21							21
22							22
23							23
24							24
25							25
26							26
27							27
28							28
29							29
30							30
31							31
32							32
33							33
34							34
35							35
36							36

PROBLEM 7-7—CONCLUDED

1.

Collection docket

Debtor	Date claim rec'd	No.
Address	Date Disposed of	
	Total Amount	
Business	Amount Collected	
Creditor	Fee	
Address	Expense	
	Amount Remitted	
Rec'd claim from	Check No.	
Attorney for debtor	Received from Creditor	
Calls on debtor	Date / For / Amount	
Correspondence		

Received from Debtor				Paid to Creditor			
Date	Amount	Date	Amount	Check No.	Amount	Check No.	Amount

Remarks

PROBLEM 7-8

1.—3.

CASH RECEIPTS JOURNAL   Page 1

DATE	DESCRIPTION	POST REF.	GENERAL CR.	REVENUE		LIAB. FOR TRUST FUNDS 221 CR.	CLIENTS TRUST ACCT. 121 DR.	CASH 111 DR.
				Legal Fees 411 CR.	Coll. Fees 421 CR.			

Total debits   _____

Total credits   _____

CASH PAYMENTS JOURNAL   Page 1

DATE	DESCRIPTION	POST REF.	GENERAL DR.	LIAB. FOR TRUST FUNDS 221 DR.	SALARY EXP. 542 DR.	EMP. INC. TAX PAY. 231 CR.	FICA TAX PAY OASDI 232 CR.	FICA TAX PAY HI 233 CR.	CHECK NO.	CLIENT'S TRUST ACCT. 121 CR.	CHECK NO.	CASH 111 CR.

Total debits   _____

Total credits   _____

PROBLEM 7-8—CONTINUED

1.   **GENERAL JOURNAL**   PAGE 1

	DATE		DESCRIPTION	POST REF.	DEBIT	CREDIT	
1							1
2							2
3							3
4							4
5							5
6							6
7							7
8							8
9							9
10							10
11							11
12							12
13							13
14							14
15							15
16							16
17							17
18							18
19							19
20							20
21							21
22							22
23							23
24							24
25							25
26							26
27							27
28							28
29							29
30							30
31							31
32							32
33							33
34							34
35							35
36							36

PROBLEM 7-8—CONCLUDED

1.

Client												No.																			

Address			
Court			
Court File No.		20	
Calendar No.		Attorney for	
Other Attorneys			
Nature of Matter			
Remarks			

	Fees and Payments	Moneys Received		Balance Due
		Purpose	Amount	

Date	Services Rendered				
	Carried Forward				

PROBLEM 7-9

1.—3.

CASH RECEIPTS JOURNAL   Page 1

DATE	DESCRIPTION	POST REF.	GENERAL CR.	REVENUE		LIAB. FOR TRUST FUNDS 221 CR.	CLIENTS TRUST ACCT. 121 DR.	CASH 111 DR.
				Legal Fees 411 CR.	Coll. Fees 421 CR.			

Total debits   _____

Total credits   _____

CASH PAYMENTS JOURNAL   Page 1

DATE	DESCRIPTION	POST REF.	GENERAL DR.	LIAB. FOR TRUST FUNDS 221 DR.	SALARY EXP. 542 DR.	EMP. INC. TAX PAY. 231 CR.	FICA TAX PAY OASDI 232 CR.	FICA TAX PAY HI 233 CR.	CHECK NO.	CLIENT'S TRUST ACCT. 121 CR.	CHECK NO.	CASH 111 CR.

Total debits   _____

Total credits   _____

PROBLEM 7-9—CONTINUED

1. GENERAL JOURNAL PAGE

	DATE	DESCRIPTION	POST REF.	DEBIT	CREDIT	
1						1
2						2
3						3
4						4
5						5
6						6
7						7
8						8
9						9
10						10
11						11
12						12
13						13
14						14
15						15
16						16
17						17
18						18
19						19
20						20
21						21
22						22
23						23
24						24
25						25
26						26
27						27
28						28
29						29
30						30
31						31
32						32
33						33
34						34
35						35
36						36

PROBLEM 7-9—CONCLUDED

1.

Collection Docket

Debtor		Date claim rec'd		No.	
Address		**Date Disposed of**			
		Total Amount			
Business		**Amount Collected**			
Creditor		**Fee**			
Address		**Expense**			
		Amount Remitted			
Rec'd claim from		**Check No.**			
Attorney for debtor		**Received from Creditor**			
Calls on debtor		Date	For	Amount	
Correspondence					

Received from Debtor				Paid to Creditor			
Date	Amount	Date	Amount	Check No.	Amount	Check No.	Amount

Remarks

CHALLENGE PROBLEM

2., 3., and 10.

CASH RECEIPTS JOURNAL   Page 14

DATE	DESCRIPTION	POST REF.	GENERAL CR.	REVENUE Legal Fees 411 CR.	REVENUE Coll. Fees 421 CR.	LIAB. FOR TRUST FUNDS 221 CR.	CLIENTS TRUST ACCT. 121 DR.	CASH 111 DR.

Total debits   _____

Total credits   _____

CHALLENGE PROBLEM—CONTINUED

2., 3., and 10.

CASH PAYMENTS JOURNAL   Page   15

DATE	DESCRIPTION	POST REF.	GENERAL DR.	LIAB. FOR TRUST FUNDS 221 DR.	SALARY EXP. 542 DR.	EMP. INC. TAX PAY. 231 CR.	FICA TAX PAY OASDI 232 CR.	FICA TAX PAY HI 233 CR.	CHECK NO.	CLIENT'S TRUST ACCT. 121 CR.	CHECK NO.	CASH 111 CR.

Total debits   _____

Total credits   _____

CHALLENGE PROBLEM—CONTINUED

2., 3., 10., and 11.   **GENERAL JOURNAL**   PAGE 3

	DATE		DESCRIPTION	POST REF.	DEBIT	CREDIT	
1							1
2							2
3							3
4							4
5							5
6							6
7							7
8							8
9							9
10							10
11							11
12							12
13							13
14							14
15							15
16							16
17							17
18							18
19							19
20							20
21							21
22							22
23							23
24							24
25							25
26							26
27							27
28							28
29							29
30							30
31							31
32							32
33							33
34							34
35							35
36							36

CHALLENGE PROBLEM—CONTINUED

2., 3., 10., and 11.   **GENERAL JOURNAL**   PAGE   4

	DATE		DESCRIPTION	POST REF.	DEBIT	CREDIT	
1							1
2							2
3							3
4							4
5							5
6							6
7							7
8							8
9							9
10							10
11							11
12							12
13							13
14							14
15							15
16							16
17							17
18							18
19							19
20							20
21							21
22							22
23							23
24							24
25							25
26							26
27							27
28							28
29							29
30							30
31							31
32							32
33							33
34							34
35							35
36							36

CHALLENGE PROBLEM—CONTINUED

2.

Collection Docket

Debtor		Date claim rec'd			No.	
Address		**Date Disposed of**				
		Total Amount				
Business		**Amount Collected**				
Creditor		**Fee**				
Address		**Expense**				
		Amount Remitted				
Rec'd claim from		**Check No.**				
Attorney for debtor		**Received from Creditor**				
Calls on debtor		Date	For	Amount		
Correspondence						

Received from Debtor				Paid to Creditor			
Date	Amount	Date	Amount	Check No.	Amount	Check No.	Amount

Remarks

CHALLENGE PROBLEM—CONTINUED

Client		
Address		No.
IN RE:	Court	
	Court File No.	
	Calendar No.	20
	Other Attorneys	Attorney for
	Nature of Matter	
	Remarks	

Date	Services Rendered	Fees and Payments	Moneys Received		Balance Due
			Purpose	Amount	
		Carried Forward			

CHALLENGE PROBLEM—CONTINUED
1.—4., 5. and 10.

General Ledger

ACCOUNT Cash   ACCOUNT NO. 111

DATE		ITEM	POST REF.	DEBIT	CREDIT	BALANCE	
						DEBIT	CREDIT

ACCOUNT Petty Cash Fund   ACCOUNT NO. 112

DATE		ITEM	POST REF.	DEBIT	CREDIT	BALANCE	
						DEBIT	CREDIT

ACCOUNT Clients Trust Account   ACCOUNT NO. 121

DATE		ITEM	POST REF.	DEBIT	CREDIT	BALANCE	
						DEBIT	CREDIT

ACCOUNT Advances On Behalf Of Clients   ACCOUNT NO. 131

DATE		ITEM	POST REF.	DEBIT	CREDIT	BALANCE	
						DEBIT	CREDIT

CHALLENGE PROBLEM—CONTINUED

ACCOUNT Office Supplies   ACCOUNT NO. 141

DATE	ITEM	POST REF.	DEBIT	CREDIT	BALANCE	
					DEBIT	CREDIT

ACCOUNT Prepaid Insurance   ACCOUNT NO. 145

DATE	ITEM	POST REF.	DEBIT	CREDIT	BALANCE	
					DEBIT	CREDIT

ACCOUNT Automobile   ACCOUNT NO. 185

DATE	ITEM	POST REF.	DEBIT	CREDIT	BALANCE	
					DEBIT	CREDIT

ACCOUNT Accumulated Depreciation—Automobile   ACCOUNT NO. 185.1

DATE	ITEM	POST REF.	DEBIT	CREDIT	BALANCE	
					DEBIT	CREDIT

CHALLENGE PROBLEM—CONTINUED

ACCOUNT Office Equipment   ACCOUNT NO. 191

DATE	ITEM	POST REF.	DEBIT	CREDIT	BALANCE	
					DEBIT	CREDIT

ACCOUNT Accumulated Depreciation—Office Equipment   ACCOUNT NO. 191.1

DATE	ITEM	POST REF.	DEBIT	CREDIT	BALANCE	
					DEBIT	CREDIT

ACCOUNT Accounts Payable   ACCOUNT NO. 211

DATE	ITEM	POST REF.	DEBIT	CREDIT	BALANCE	
					DEBIT	CREDIT

ACCOUNT Liability for Trust Funds   ACCOUNT NO. 221

DATE	ITEM	POST REF.	DEBIT	CREDIT	BALANCE	
					DEBIT	CREDIT

CHALLENGE PROBLEM—CONTINUED

ACCOUNT Employees Income Tax Payable   ACCOUNT NO. 231

DATE	ITEM	POST REF.	DEBIT	CREDIT	BALANCE	
					DEBIT	CREDIT

ACCOUNT FICA Tax Payable—OASDI   ACCOUNT NO. 232

DATE	ITEM	POST REF.	DEBIT	CREDIT	BALANCE	
					DEBIT	CREDIT

ACCOUNT FICA Tax Payable—HI   ACCOUNT NO. 233

DATE	ITEM	POST REF.	DEBIT	CREDIT	BALANCE	
					DEBIT	CREDIT

ACCOUNT Suzanne Womack, Capital   ACCOUNT NO. 311

DATE	ITEM	POST REF.	DEBIT	CREDIT	BALANCE	
					DEBIT	CREDIT

CHALLENGE PROBLEM—CONTINUED

ACCOUNT Suzanne Womack, Drawing   ACCOUNT NO. 312

DATE		ITEM	POST REF.	DEBIT	CREDIT	BALANCE	
						DEBIT	CREDIT

ACCOUNT Income Summary   ACCOUNT NO. 331

DATE		ITEM	POST REF.	DEBIT	CREDIT	BALANCE	
						DEBIT	CREDIT

ACCOUNT Legal Fees Revenue   ACCOUNT NO. 411

DATE		ITEM	POST REF.	DEBIT	CREDIT	BALANCE	
						DEBIT	CREDIT

ACCOUNT Collection Fees Revenue   ACCOUNT NO. 421

DATE		ITEM	POST REF.	DEBIT	CREDIT	BALANCE	
						DEBIT	CREDIT

CHALLENGE PROBLEM—CONTINUED

ACCOUNT Rent Expense   ACCOUNT NO. 541

DATE	ITEM	POST REF.	DEBIT	CREDIT	BALANCE	
					DEBIT	CREDIT

ACCOUNT Salary Expense   ACCOUNT NO. 542

DATE	ITEM	POST REF.	DEBIT	CREDIT	BALANCE	
					DEBIT	CREDIT

ACCOUNT Office Supplies Expense   ACCOUNT NO. 543

DATE	ITEM	POST REF.	DEBIT	CREDIT	BALANCE	
					DEBIT	CREDIT

ACCOUNT Telephone Expense   ACCOUNT NO. 545

DATE	ITEM	POST REF.	DEBIT	CREDIT	BALANCE	
					DEBIT	CREDIT

CHALLENGE PROBLEM—CONTINUED

ACCOUNT Automobile Expense   ACCOUNT NO. 546

DATE	ITEM	POST REF.	DEBIT	CREDIT	BALANCE	
					DEBIT	CREDIT

ACCOUNT Depreciation Expense—Automobile   ACCOUNT NO. 547

DATE	ITEM	POST REF.	DEBIT	CREDIT	BALANCE	
					DEBIT	CREDIT

ACCOUNT Depreciation Expense—Office Equipment   ACCOUNT NO. 548

DATE	ITEM	POST REF.	DEBIT	CREDIT	BALANCE	
					DEBIT	CREDIT

ACCOUNT Insurance Expense   ACCOUNT NO. 549

DATE	ITEM	POST REF.	DEBIT	CREDIT	BALANCE	
					DEBIT	CREDIT

CHALLENGE PROBLEM—CONTINUED

ACCOUNT Law Library Expense   ACCOUNT NO. 551

DATE	ITEM	POST REF.	DEBIT	CREDIT	BALANCE	
					DEBIT	CREDIT

ACCOUNT Payroll Taxes Expense   ACCOUNT NO. 552

DATE	ITEM	POST REF.	DEBIT	CREDIT	BALANCE	
					DEBIT	CREDIT

ACCOUNT Charitable Contributions Expense   ACCOUNT NO. 557

DATE	ITEM	POST REF.	DEBIT	CREDIT	BALANCE	
					DEBIT	CREDIT

ACCOUNT Miscellaneous Expense   ACCOUNT NO. 572

DATE	ITEM	POST REF.	DEBIT	CREDIT	BALANCE	
					DEBIT	CREDIT

CHALLENGE PROBLEM—CONTINUED

6.

Suzanne Woamck, Attorney at Law

Trial Balance

December 31, 200X

This page not used.

CHALLENGE PROBLEM—CONTINUED
6.—10.

Suzanne Womack, Attorney at Law
Work Sheet
For the Year Ended December 31, 200X

Account Title	Trial Balance		Adjustments	
	Debit	Credit	Debit	Credit

CHALLENGE PROBLEM—CONTINUED

Suzanne Womack, Attorney at Law
Work Sheet
For the Year Ended December 31, 200X

Adjusted Trial Balance		Income Statement		Balance Sheet	
Debit	Credit	Debit	Credit	Debit	Credit

CHALLENGE PROBLEM—CONTINUED

9.

Suzanne Womack, Attorney at Law

Income Statement

For the Year Ended December 31, 200X

Suzanne Womack, Attorney at Law

Statement of Owner's Equity

For the Year Ended December 31, 200X

CHALLENGE PROBLEM—CONTINUED

Suzanne Womack, Attorney at Law

Balance Sheet

December 31, 200X

CHALLENGE PROBLEM—CONTINUED

Suzanne Womack, Attorney at Law

Post Closing Trial Balance

December 31, 200X

CHAPTER 8

ACCOUNTING FOR PHYSICIANS AND DENTISTS

PRACTICE TEST

Part I—True/False

Please circle the correct answer.

T F 1. Under the accrual basis of accounting, revenue and expenses are recognized when cash is received or paid.

T F 2. Under a modified cash basis of accounting, revenue and expenses are recognized only when cash is received or paid, and adjusting entries are made for prepaid assets and long-term assets.

T F 3. Most physicians and dentists use the accrual basis of accounting.

T F 4. A cash receipts journal is used as the book of original entry for all cash that is paid by the business.

T F 5. A daily service record is set up as a double-entry record where total debits must equal total credits.

T F 6. In the daily service record, the total of the office visits and surgery columns must equal the total of the patients charges and cash services columns.

T F 7. The patients' accounts are kept on ledger cards and collectively they are known as the patients ledger.

T F 8. Accepting assignments means that the patient will pay only those amounts due that are not covered by insurance.

T F 9. Posting from the cash receipts journal and cash payments journal involves both summary posting and individual posting.

T F 10. To indicate that the total of the General Dr. column of the Cash Payments Journal is not posted, a check mark is written in parentheses below the column total.

Part II—Multiple Choice

Please circle the correct answer.

1. The basis of accounting that recognizes revenue and expenses when earned or incurred, regardless of when cash is received or paid is called the
    a. Accrual basis
    b. Cash basis
    c. Modified cash basis
    d. All the above

2. The basis of accounting that recognizes revenue and expenses only when cash is received or paid is called the
    a. Accrual basis
    b. Cash basis
    c. Accounting basis
    d. Revenue and expense basis

Part II—Continued

3.   The basis of accounting that recognizes revenue and expenses only when cash is received or paid and allows for adjusting entries on long-term assets and prepaid assets is called the
        a.   Accrual basis
        b.   Cash basis
        c.   Modified cash basis
        d.   Both (b) and (c)

4.   The basis of accounting that most physicians and dentists use is the
        a.   Accrual basis
        b.   Cash basis
        c.   Modified cash basis
        d.   All the above

5.   A cash receipts journal for a physician or dentist would include a
        a.   Cash Credit column
        b.   Other Income debit column
        c.   Professional Fees credit column
        d.   All the above

6.   A cash payments journal for a physician or dentist would include a
        a.   Cash Debit column
        b.   General Debit column
        c.   Salary Expense Credit column
        d.   Employees Income Tax Payable debit column

7.   Posting from either the cash receipts journal or cash payments journal would include
        a.   Summary posting
        b.   Individual posting
        c.   Both summary and individual posting
        d.   Individual posting only

8.   In the daily service record, the total of the office visits and surgery columns must equal the total of the
        a.   Patients Charges and Cash Service columns
        b.   Patients Payments and Cash Services columns
        c.   Office Visits and Cash Services columns
        d.   Surgery and Cash Services columns

9.   In the daily service record, each entry under the Kinds of Services columns must also be entered in either the Patients Accounts Charges or the
        a.   Office Visits column
        b.   Surgery column
        c.   Cash Services column
        d.   None of the above

10.   A doctor or a dentist may allow the patient to pay only those amounts due that are not covered by insurance. This is called
        a.   Accepting insurance
        b.   Deferring payment
        c.   Crediting accounts
        d.   Accepting assignments

Part III—Fill in the Blank

1.   The _____ basis of accounting recognizes revenue and expenses when earned or incurred, regardless of when cash is received or paid.

2.   The basis of accounting that recognizes revenue and expenses only when cash is received or paid, with no adjustments for depreciation of long-term assets or for the usage of supplies and other prepaid assets, is called the _____ basis.

3.   The basis of accounting that recognizes revenue and expenses only when cash is received or paid, but allows for year-end adjustments for depreciation of long-term assets and other prepaid assets, is called the _____ basis.

4.   A _____ is used as the book of original entry for all cash that is received by the business.

5.   A _____. is used as the book of original entry for all payments of cash.

6.   Posting from either the cash receipts journal or the cash payments journal includes posting by column totals, called _____ , and posting from the general debit column, called _____.

7.   To indicate that the total of the General Dr. column is not posted, a _____ is written in parentheses below the total.

8.   A _____ is used to record the kinds of services, patient accounts, and cash services.

9.   The patients' accounts are kept on ledger cards and collectively they are known as the _____.

10.   The _____ was developed by the American Medical Association and is used by most insurance carriers and programs.

Part IV—Practice Problems

Practice Problem 1—Calculation of Insurance Coverage

Rick Goss incurred medical expenses of $6,430. All the charges were covered by his insurance. The deductible on his policy is $200 and the coverage that his insurance company will pay is 80%.

Required:

1. How much of the debt will the insurance company?
2. How much of the debt must Rich pay?

Work Space:

Practice Problem 2—Preparing Journal Entries, Using Special Journals

Evan Thomas, M.D., physician and surgeon, employs Ruth Ridgway as an office assistant. A partial chart of accounts and selected transactions for the month of February 200X are listed below.

EVAN THOMAS, PHYSICIAN AND SURGEON
Partial Chart Of Accounts

ASSETS
- 111 Cash
- 112 Petty Cash Fund
- 113 Office Supplies
- 115 Prepaid Insurance
- 191 Office Equipment

LIABILITIES
- 211 Accounts Payable
- 231 Employees' Income Tax Payable
- 232 FICA Tax Payable—OASDI
- 233 FICA Tax Payable—HI
- 241 FUTA Tax Payable
- 251 SUTA Tax Payable

OWNER'S EQUITY
- 311 Evan Thomas, Capital
- 312 Evan Thomas, Drawing

REVENUE
- 411 Professional Fees
- 421 Other Income

EXPENSES
- 512 Charitable Contributions Expense
- 516 Dues and Subscriptions Expense
- 521 Laundry Expense
- 523 Legal Expense
- 527 Medical Library Expense
- 528 Medical Supplies Expense
- 532 Payroll Taxes Expense
- 535 Postage Expense
- 543 Repairs and Maintenance Expense
- 551 Salary Expense
- 553 Surgical Instruments Expense
- 567 Traveling and Meetings Expense
- 581 Miscellaneous Expense

Feb.   3   Received $800 for speaking at a medical society meeting.

5   Paid $3,300 for liability insurance for the next six months. Issued check no. 332.

7   Total cash received from patients for the week ended February 7 was:

Payments	$5,255
Cash Services	915
Total	$6,170

12   Paid $125 for a new medical research book. Issued check no. 333.

14   Paid Ruth Ridgway, employee's wages of $1,100, less income tax payable $130, less FICA tax Payable—OASDI $68.20, less FICA tax payable—HI $15.95. Issued check no. 334 for $885.85.

14   Total cash received from patients for the week ended February 14 was:

Payments	$4,170
Cash Services	990
Total	$5,160

14   Paid January payroll taxes to Columbia National Bank as follows. Issued check no. 335.

Employee's income tax withheld	$260.00
FICA tax payable—OASDI	272.80
FICA tax payable—HI	63.80
Total amount of check	$596.60

Practice Problem 2—Continued

17 Paid $525 for surgical supplies. Issued check no. 336.

18 Paid $315 for medical supplies. Issued check no. 337.

21 Paid $820 for surgical instruments. Issued check no. 338.

21 Total cash received from patients for the week ended February 21 was:

Payments...$4,825

Cash Services...__780__

Total..$5,605

25 Paid $710 for legal expenses. Issued check no. 339

26 Paid $135 for laundry expense. Issued check no. 340.

28 Total cash received from patients for the week ended February 28 was:

Payments...$3,690

Cash Services...__810__

Total..$4,500

28 Paid Ruth Ridgway, employee's wages of $1,100, less income tax payable $130, less FICA tax payable—OASDI, $68.20, less FICA tax payable—HI, $15.95. Issued check no. 334 for $885.85.

27 Replenished the petty cash fund. Issued check no. 343. The following payments had been made:

Dues and Subscriptions Expense $40.00

Postage Expense... 29.00

Repairs and Maintenance Expense............... 25.00

Required:

1. Record the foregoing transactions in the cash receipts and cash payments journals.
2. Foot and prove the totals of the journals.

CASH RECEIPTS JOURNAL   Page   1

DATE	DESCRIPTION	POST REF.	GENERAL DR.	OTHER INCOME 411 CR	PROFESSIONAL FEES 412 CR.	CASH 111 DR.

Total debits   _____

Total credits   _____

Practice Problem 2—Concluded

CASH PAYMENTS JOURNAL

Page 1

DATE	CHECK NO.	DESCRIPTION	POST REF.	GENERAL DR.	SALARY EXPENSE 551 DR.	EMP. INC. TAX PAY. 231 CR.	FICA TAX PAY. OASDI 232 CR.	FICA TAX PAY. HI 233 CR	CASH 111 CR

Total debits _____

Total credits _____

SOLUTIONS TO PRACTICE TEST

Part I	Part II	Part III
1. F	1. a	1. accrual
2. T	2. b	2. cash
3. F	3. c	3. modified cash
4. F	4. c	4. cash receipts journal
5. F	5. c	5. cash payments journal
6. T	6. b	6. summary posting, individual posting
7. T	7. c	7. check mark
8. T	8. a	8. daily service record
9. T	9. c	9. patients ledger
10. T	10. d	10. Universal Health Insurance Claim Form

Part IV

Practice Problem 1

1. $6,430 − $200 = $6,230 × 80% = $4,984
2. $200 + $1,246 ($6,230 × 20%) = $1,446

Practice Problem 2

CASH RECEIPTS JOURNAL   Page   1

DATE		DESCRIPTION	POST REF.	GENERAL DR.	OTHER INCOME 421 CR	PROFESSIONAL FEES 411 CR.	CASH 111 DR.
200X Feb.	3	Speaking Engagement			800.00		800.00
	7	Total Receipts				6,170.00	6,170.00
	14	Total Receipts				5,160.00	5,160.00
	21	Total Receipts				5,605.00	5,605.00
	28	Total Receipts				4,500.00	4,500.00
				00.00	800.00	21,435.00	22,235.00

Total debits   22,235.00

Total credits   22,235.00

Practice Problem 2—Concluded

CASH PAYMENTS JOURNAL   Page 1

DATE		CHECK NO.	DESCRIPTION	POST REF.	GENERAL DR.	SALARY EXPENSE 551 DR.	EMP. INC. TAX PAY. 231 CR.	FICA TAX PAY. OASDI 232 CR.	FICA TAX PAY. HI 233 CR	CASH 111 CR
200X Feb.	5	332	Prepaid Insurance		3,300.00					3,300.00
	12	333	Medical Library Expense		125.00					125.00
	14	334	Ruth Ridgway			1,100.00	130.00	68.20	15.95	885.85
	14	335	Employee's Inc. Tax Payment		260.00					
			FICA Tax Payable—OASDI		272.80					
			FICA Tax Payable—HI		63.80					596.60
	17	336	Surgical Supplies Expense		525.00					525.00
	18	337	Medical Supplies Expense		315.00					315.00
	21	338	Surgical Instruments Expense		820.00					820.00
	25	339	Legal Expense		710.00					710.00
	26	340	Laundry Expense		135.00					135.00
	28	341	Ruth Ridgway			1,100.00	130.00	68.20	15.95	885.85
	28	343	Dues and Subscriptions Exp.		40.00					
			Postage Expense		29.00					
			Repairs and Maint. Expense		25.00					94.00
					6,620.60	2,200.00	260.00	136.40	31.90	8,392.30

Total debits   8,820.60

Total credits   8,820.60

CHAPTER 8 WORKING PAPERS
EXERCISE 8-1

1. and 2.

_____

_____

_____

_____

_____

_____

EXERCISE 8-2

STATEMENT

JOHN S. RHODES, M.D.   MARIA L. DOMINGO, M. D.

RHODES & DOMINGO
56 Schuler St., NE, Portland, OR 97217-9567
555-8134

**Bea Goss
6241 East Wales Boulevard
Portland, OR 97208-6431**

Date	Professional Service	Charge	Paid	Balance

PAY LAST AMOUNT IN THIS COLUMN ⇑

1603
CBC – Complete Blood Count
CK – Check
CPX – Complete Physical
EKG – Electrocardiagram
ER – Emergency Room
HOSP – Hospital Visit

I – Injection
INS – Insurance
OV – Office Visit
S – Surgery
X – X-ray
MISC – Miscellaneous

EXERCISE 8-3

GENERAL JOURNAL

	DATE		DESCRIPTION	POST REF.	DEBIT	CREDIT	
1							1
2							2
3							3
4							4
5							5
6							6
7							7
8							8
9							9
10							10
11							11
12							12
13							13
14							14
15							15
16							16
17							17
18							18
19							19
20							20
21							21
22							22
23							23
24							24
25							25
26							26
27							27
28							28
29							29
30							30
31							31
32							32
33							33
34							34
35							35
36							36

EXERCISE 8-4

CASH RECEIPTS JOURNAL   Page   1

DATE	DESCRIPTION	POST REF.	GENERAL DR.	PROFESSIONAL FEES 411 CR.	CASH 111 DR.

CASH PAYMENTS JOURNAL   Page   1

DATE	CHECK NO.	DESCRIPTION	POST REF.	GENERAL DR.	SALARY EXPENSE 551 DR.	EMP. INC. TAX PAY. 231 CR.	FICA TAX PAY. OASDI 232 CR.	FICA TAX PAY. HI 233 CR	CASH 111 CR

PROBLEM 8-5

1. and 2.

CASH RECEIPTS JOURNAL   Page   23

DATE	DESCRIPTION	POST REF.	GENERAL DR.	PROF. FEES DENTISTRY 421 CR	PROF. FEES ORAL HYGIENE 411 CR.	CASH 111 DR.

Total debits   _____

Total credits   _____

PROBLEM 8-5—CONTINUED
1. and 2.

CASH PAYMENTS JOURNAL   Page 31

DATE	CHECK NO.	DESCRIPTION	POST REF.	GENERAL DR.	SALARY EXPENSE 551 DR.	EMP. INC. TAX PAY. 231 CR.	FICA TAX PAY. OASDI 232 CR.	FICA TAX PAY. HI 233 CR	CASH 111 CR

Total debits   _____

Total credits   _____

PROBLEM 8-5—CONTINUED

1. **GENERAL JOURNAL** PAGE 13

	DATE		DESCRIPTION	POST REF.	DEBIT	CREDIT	
1							1
2							2
3							3
4							4
5							5
6							6
7							7
8							8
9							9
10							10
11							11
12							12
13							13
14							14
15							15
16							16
17							17
18							18
19							19
20							20
21							21
22							22
23							23
24							24
25							25
26							26
27							27
28							28
29							29
30							30
31							31
32							32
33							33
34							34
35							35
36							36

PROBLEM 8-5—CONTINUED

3.

General Ledger

ACCOUNT Cash   ACCOUNT NO. 111

DATE	ITEM	POST REF.	DEBIT	CREDIT	BALANCE DEBIT	BALANCE CREDIT

ACCOUNT Office Supplies   ACCOUNT NO. 113

DATE	ITEM	POST REF.	DEBIT	CREDIT	BALANCE DEBIT	BALANCE CREDIT

ACCOUNT Professional Supplies   ACCOUNT NO. 114

DATE	ITEM	POST REF.	DEBIT	CREDIT	BALANCE DEBIT	BALANCE CREDIT

ACCOUNT Professional Equipment   ACCOUNT NO. 161

DATE	ITEM	POST REF.	DEBIT	CREDIT	BALANCE DEBIT	BALANCE CREDIT

PROBLEM 8-5—CONTINUED

ACCOUNT Accumulated Depreciation—Professional Equipment   ACCOUNT NO. 161.1

DATE	ITEM	POST REF.	DEBIT	CREDIT	BALANCE DEBIT	BALANCE CREDIT

ACCOUNT Office Equipment   ACCOUNT NO. 171

DATE	ITEM	POST REF.	DEBIT	CREDIT	BALANCE DEBIT	BALANCE CREDIT

ACCOUNT Accumulated Depreciation—Office Equipment   ACCOUNT NO. 171.1

DATE	ITEM	POST REF.	DEBIT	CREDIT	BALANCE DEBIT	BALANCE CREDIT

ACCOUNT Employees' Income Tax Payable   ACCOUNT NO. 231

DATE	ITEM	POST REF.	DEBIT	CREDIT	BALANCE DEBIT	BALANCE CREDIT

PROBLEM 8-5—CONTINUED

ACCOUNT FICA Tax Payable—OASDI

ACCOUNT NO. 232

DATE		ITEM	POST REF.	DEBIT	CREDIT	BALANCE	
						DEBIT	CREDIT

ACCOUNT FICA Tax Payable—HI

ACCOUNT NO. 233

DATE		ITEM	POST REF.	DEBIT	CREDIT	BALANCE	
						DEBIT	CREDIT

ACCOUNT FUTA Tax Payable

ACCOUNT NO. 241

DATE		ITEM	POST REF.	DEBIT	CREDIT	BALANCE	
						DEBIT	CREDIT

ACCOUNT SUTA Tax Payable

ACCOUNT NO. 251

DATE		ITEM	POST REF.	DEBIT	CREDIT	BALANCE	
						DEBIT	CREDIT

PROBLEM 8-5—CONTINUED

ACCOUNT Jeanine Herzog, Capital   ACCOUNT NO. 311

DATE	ITEM	POST REF.	DEBIT	CREDIT	BALANCE DEBIT	BALANCE CREDIT

ACCOUNT Jeanine Herzog, Drawing   ACCOUNT NO. 312

DATE	ITEM	POST REF.	DEBIT	CREDIT	BALANCE DEBIT	BALANCE CREDIT

ACCOUNT Professional Fees—Dentistry   ACCOUNT NO. 411

DATE	ITEM	POST REF.	DEBIT	CREDIT	BALANCE DEBIT	BALANCE CREDIT

ACCOUNT Professional Fees—Oral Hygiene   ACCOUNT NO. 412

DATE	ITEM	POST REF.	DEBIT	CREDIT	BALANCE DEBIT	BALANCE CREDIT

PROBLEM 8-5—CONTINUED

ACCOUNT Laboratory Expense   ACCOUNT NO. 511

DATE	ITEM	POST REF.	DEBIT	CREDIT	BALANCE	
					DEBIT	CREDIT

ACCOUNT Laundry Expense   ACCOUNT NO. 512

DATE	ITEM	POST REF.	DEBIT	CREDIT	BALANCE	
					DEBIT	CREDIT

ACCOUNT Payroll Taxes Expense   ACCOUNT NO. 532

DATE	ITEM	POST REF.	DEBIT	CREDIT	BALANCE	
					DEBIT	CREDIT

ACCOUNT Rent Expense   ACCOUNT NO. 541

DATE	ITEM	POST REF.	DEBIT	CREDIT	BALANCE	
					DEBIT	CREDIT

PROBLEM 8-5—CONTINUED

ACCOUNT Salary Expense   ACCOUNT NO. 551

DATE	ITEM	POST REF.	DEBIT	CREDIT	BALANCE	
					DEBIT	CREDIT

ACCOUNT Telephone Expense   ACCOUNT NO. 561

DATE	ITEM	POST REF.	DEBIT	CREDIT	BALANCE	
					DEBIT	CREDIT

ACCOUNT Utilities Expense   ACCOUNT NO. 567

DATE	ITEM	POST REF.	DEBIT	CREDIT	BALANCE	
					DEBIT	CREDIT

ACCOUNT Miscellaneous Expense   ACCOUNT NO. 581

DATE	ITEM	POST REF.	DEBIT	CREDIT	BALANCE	
					DEBIT	CREDIT

PROBLEM 8-5—CONCLUDED

Dr. Jeanine Herzog, Dentist
Trial Balance
April 30, 200X

Account Name	Debit	Credit
Cash		
Office Supplies		
Professional Supplies		
Professional Equipment		
Accumulated Depreciation—Professional Equipment		
Office Equipment		
Accumulated Depreciation—Office Equipment		
Employees' Income Tax Payable		
FICA Tax Payable—OASDI		
FICA Tax Payable—HI		
FUTA Tax Payable		
SUTA Tax Payable		
Jeanine Herzog, Capital		
Jeanine Herzog, Drawing		
Professional Fees—Dentistry		
Professional Fees—Oral Hygiene		
Laboratory Expense		
Laundry Expense		
Payroll Taxes Expense		
Rent Expense		
Salary Expense		
Telephone Expense		
Utilities Expense		
Miscellaneous Expense		

PROBLEM 8-6
2., 3., and 4.

CASH RECEIPTS JOURNAL   Page 19

DATE		DESCRIPTION	POST REF.	GENERAL DR.	PROFESSIONAL FEES 411 CR.	CASH 111 DR.

CASH PAYMENTS JOURNAL   Page 23

DATE	CHECK NO.	DESCRIPTION	POST REF.	GENERAL DR.	SALARY EXPENSE 551 DR.	EMP. INC. TAX PAY. 231 CR.	FICA TAX PAY. OASDI 232 CR.	FICA TAX PAY. HI 233 CR	CASH 111 CR

Total debits _____

Total credits _____

PROBLEM 8-6—CONTINUED

9.

GENERAL JOURNAL

	DATE		DESCRIPTION	POST REF.	DEBIT	CREDIT	
1							1
2							2
3							3
4							4
5							5
6							6
7							7
8							8
9							9
10							10
11							11
12							12
13							13
14							14
15							15
16							16
17							17
18							18
19							19
20							20
21							21
22							22
23							23
24							24
25							25
26							26
27							27
28							28
29							29
30							30
31							31
32							32
33							33
34							34
35							35
36							36

PROBLEM 8-6—CONTINUED

10.

GENERAL JOURNAL

	DATE	DESCRIPTION	POST REF.	DEBIT	CREDIT	
1						1
2						2
3						3
4						4
5						5
6						6
7						7
8						8
9						9
10						10
11						11
12						12
13						13
14						14
15						15
16						16
17						17
18						18
19						19
20						20
21						21
22						22
23						23
24						24
25						25
26						26
27						27
28						28
29						29
30						30
31						31
32						32
33						33
34						34
35						35
36						36

PROBLEM 8-6—CONTINUED
General Ledger

1. and 4.

ACCOUNT Cash ACCOUNT NO. 111

DATE	ITEM	POST REF.	DEBIT	CREDIT	BALANCE DEBIT	BALANCE CREDIT

ACCOUNT Medical Supplies ACCOUNT NO. 114

DATE	ITEM	POST REF.	DEBIT	CREDIT	BALANCE DEBIT	BALANCE CREDIT

ACCOUNT Prepaid Insurance ACCOUNT NO. 118

DATE	ITEM	POST REF.	DEBIT	CREDIT	BALANCE DEBIT	BALANCE CREDIT

ACCOUNT Medical Equipment ACCOUNT NO. 161

DATE	ITEM	POST REF.	DEBIT	CREDIT	BALANCE DEBIT	BALANCE CREDIT

PROBLEM 8-6—CONTINUED

ACCOUNT Accumulated Depreciation—Medical Equipment   ACCOUNT NO. 161.1

DATE	ITEM	POST REF.	DEBIT	CREDIT	BALANCE	
					DEBIT	CREDIT

ACCOUNT Office Equipment   ACCOUNT NO. 171

DATE	ITEM	POST REF.	DEBIT	CREDIT	BALANCE	
					DEBIT	CREDIT

ACCOUNT Accumulated Depreciation—Office Equipment   ACCOUNT NO. 171.1

DATE	ITEM	POST REF.	DEBIT	CREDIT	BALANCE	
					DEBIT	CREDIT

ACCOUNT Employees' Income Tax Payable   ACCOUNT NO. 231

DATE	ITEM	POST REF.	DEBIT	CREDIT	BALANCE	
					DEBIT	CREDIT

PROBLEM 8-6—CONTINUED

ACCOUNT FICA Tax Payable—OASDI   ACCOUNT NO. 232

DATE		ITEM	POST REF.	DEBIT	CREDIT	BALANCE	
						DEBIT	CREDIT

ACCOUNT FICA Tax Payable—HI   ACCOUNT NO. 233

DATE		ITEM	POST REF.	DEBIT	CREDIT	BALANCE	
						DEBIT	CREDIT

ACCOUNT Deb Guerrero, Capital   ACCOUNT NO. 311

DATE		ITEM	POST REF.	DEBIT	CREDIT	BALANCE	
						DEBIT	CREDIT

PROBLEM 8-6—CONTINUED

ACCOUNT Deb Guerrero, Drawing   ACCOUNT NO. 312

DATE	ITEM	POST REF.	DEBIT	CREDIT	BALANCE	
					DEBIT	CREDIT

ACCOUNT Income Summary   ACCOUNT NO. 331

DATE	ITEM	POST REF.	DEBIT	CREDIT	BALANCE	
					DEBIT	CREDIT

ACCOUNT Professional Fees   ACCOUNT NO. 411

DATE	ITEM	POST REF.	DEBIT	CREDIT	BALANCE	
					DEBIT	CREDIT

ACCOUNT Laundry Expense   ACCOUNT NO. 512

DATE	ITEM	POST REF.	DEBIT	CREDIT	BALANCE	
					DEBIT	CREDIT

PROBLEM 8-6—CONTINUED

ACCOUNT Payroll Taxes Expense   ACCOUNT NO. 532

DATE	ITEM	POST REF.	DEBIT	CREDIT	BALANCE	
					DEBIT	CREDIT

ACCOUNT Rent Expense   ACCOUNT NO. 541

DATE	ITEM	POST REF.	DEBIT	CREDIT	BALANCE	
					DEBIT	CREDIT

ACCOUNT Medical Supplies Expense   ACCOUNT NO. 543

DATE	ITEM	POST REF.	DEBIT	CREDIT	BALANCE	
					DEBIT	CREDIT

ACCOUNT Depreciation Expense—Medical Equipment   ACCOUNT NO. 547

DATE	ITEM	POST REF.	DEBIT	CREDIT	BALANCE	
					DEBIT	CREDIT

PROBLEM 8-6—CONTINUED

ACCOUNT Depreciation Expense—Office Equipment ACCOUNT NO. 548

DATE	ITEM	POST REF.	DEBIT	CREDIT	BALANCE	
					DEBIT	CREDIT

ACCOUNT Insurance Expense ACCOUNT NO. 549

DATE	ITEM	POST REF.	DEBIT	CREDIT	BALANCE	
					DEBIT	CREDIT

ACCOUNT Salary Expense ACCOUNT NO. 551

DATE	ITEM	POST REF.	DEBIT	CREDIT	BALANCE	
					DEBIT	CREDIT

ACCOUNT Telephone Expense ACCOUNT NO. 561

DATE	ITEM	POST REF.	DEBIT	CREDIT	BALANCE	
					DEBIT	CREDIT

PROBLEM 8-6—CONTINUED

ACCOUNT Legal Expense   ACCOUNT NO. 564

DATE	ITEM	POST REF.	DEBIT	CREDIT	BALANCE	
					DEBIT	CREDIT

ACCOUNT Utilities Expense   ACCOUNT NO. 567

DATE	ITEM	POST REF.	DEBIT	CREDIT	BALANCE	
					DEBIT	CREDIT

ACCOUNT Miscellaneous Expense   ACCOUNT NO. 581

DATE	ITEM	POST REF.	DEBIT	CREDIT	BALANCE	
					DEBIT	CREDIT

PROBLEM 8-6—CONTINUED

6., 7., and 8.

Dr. Deb Guerrero

Work Sheet

For the Year Ended December 31, 200X

	ACCOUNT TITLE	TRIAL BALANCE DEBIT	TRIAL BALANCE CREDIT	ADJUSTMENTS DEBIT	ADJUSTMENTS CREDIT
1	Cash				
2	Medical Supplies				
3	Prepaid Insurance				
4	Medical Equipment				
5	Accum. Depr.—Medical Equipment				
6	Office Equipment				
7	Accum. Depr.—Office Equipment				
8	Employees' Income Tax Pay.				
9	FICA Tax Payable—OASDI				
10	FICA Tax Payable—HI				
11	Deb Guerrero, Capital				
12	Deb Guerrero, Drawing				
13	Professional Fees				
14	Laundry Expense				
15	Payroll Taxes Expense				
16	Rent Expense				
17	Medical Supplies Expense				
18	Depr. Exp.—Medical Equip.				
19	Depr. Exp.—Office Equip.				
20	Insurance Expense				
21	Salary Expense				
22	Telephone Expense				
23	Legal Expense				
24	Utilities Expense				
25	Miscellaneous Expense				
26					
27					
28					
29					
30					
31					
32					
33					

PROBLEM 8-6—CONTINUED

6., 7., and 8.

Dr. Deb Guerrero

Work Sheet

For the Year Ended December 31, 200X

	ADJUSTED TRIAL BALANCE		INCOME STATEMENT		BALANCE SHEET		
	DEBIT	CREDIT	DEBIT	CREDIT	DEBIT	CREDIT	
							1
							2
							3
							4
							5
							6
							7
							8
							9
							10
							11
							12
							13
							14
							15
							16
							17
							18
							19
							20
							21
							22
							23
							24
							25
							26
							27
							28
							29
							30
							31
							32
							33

PROBLEM 8-6—CONTINUED

5.

Dr. Deb Guerrero, Physician and Surgeon

Trial Balance

For the Year Ended December 31, 200X

PROBLEM 8-6—CONTINUED

5.

Dr. Deb Guerrero, Physician and Surgeon

Income Statement

For the Year Ended December 31, 200X

Dr. Deb Guerrero, Physician and Surgeon

Statement of Owner's Equity

For the Year Ended December 31, 200X

PROBLEM 8-6—CONTINUED

8.

Dr. Deb Guerrero, Physician and Surgeon
Balance Sheet
December 31, 200X

PROBLEM 8-6—CONCLUDED

11.

Dr. Deb Guerrero

Post-Closing Trial Balance

December 31, 200X

Account Name	Debit	Credit
Cash		
Medical Supplies		
Prepaid Insurance		
Medical Equipment		
Accumulated Depreciation—Medical Equipment		
Office Equipment		
Accumulated Depreciation—Office Equipment		
Employees' Income Tax Payable		
FICA Tax Payable—OASDI		
FICA Tax Payable—HI		
Deb Guerrero, Capital		

PROBLEM 8-7

1. and 2.

CASH RECEIPTS JOURNAL   Page 21

DATE	DESCRIPTION	POST REF.	GENERAL DR.	PROF. FEES DENTISTRY 412 CR.R	PROF. FEES ORAL HYGIENE 412 CR.	CASH 111 DR.

Total debits   _____

Total credits   _____

PROBLEM 8-7—CONTINUED
1. and 2.

CASH PAYMENTS JOURNAL   Page   28

DATE	CHECK NO.	DESCRIPTION	POST REF.	GENERAL DR.	SALARY EXPENSE 551 DR.	EMP. INC. TAX PAY. 231 CR.	FICA TAX PAY. OASDI 232 CR.	FICA TAX PAY. HI 233 CR	CASH 111 CR

Total debits   _____

Total credits   _____

PROBLEM 8-7—CONTINUED

1. and 2.   **GENERAL JOURNAL**

	DATE		DESCRIPTION	POST REF.	DEBIT	CREDIT	
1							1
2							2
3							3
4							4
5							5
6							6
7							7
8							8
9							9
10							10
11							11
12							12
13							13
14							14
15							15
16							16
17							17
18							18
19							19
20							20
21							21
22							22
23							23
24							24
25							25
26							26
27							27
28							28
29							29
30							30
31							31
32							32
33							33
34							34
35							35

PROBLEM 8-7—CONTINUED

3.

General Ledger

ACCOUNT Cash   ACCOUNT NO. 111

DATE	ITEM	POST REF.	DEBIT	CREDIT	BALANCE	
					DEBIT	CREDIT

ACCOUNT Office Supplies   ACCOUNT NO. 113

DATE	ITEM	POST REF.	DEBIT	CREDIT	BALANCE	
					DEBIT	CREDIT

ACCOUNT Professional Supplies   ACCOUNT NO. 114

DATE	ITEM	POST REF.	DEBIT	CREDIT	BALANCE	
					DEBIT	CREDIT

ACCOUNT Professional Equipment   ACCOUNT NO. 161

DATE	ITEM	POST REF.	DEBIT	CREDIT	BALANCE	
					DEBIT	CREDIT

PROBLEM 8-7—CONTINUED

ACCOUNT Accumulated Depreciation—Professional Equipment   ACCOUNT NO. 161.1

DATE	ITEM	POST REF.	DEBIT	CREDIT	BALANCE DEBIT	CREDIT

ACCOUNT Office Equipment   ACCOUNT NO. 171

DATE	ITEM	POST REF.	DEBIT	CREDIT	BALANCE DEBIT	CREDIT

ACCOUNT Accumulated Depreciation—Office Equipment   ACCOUNT NO. 171.1

DATE	ITEM	POST REF.	DEBIT	CREDIT	BALANCE DEBIT	CREDIT

ACCOUNT Employees' Income Tax Payable   ACCOUNT NO. 231

DATE	ITEM	POST REF.	DEBIT	CREDIT	BALANCE DEBIT	CREDIT

PROBLEM 8-7—CONTINUED

ACCOUNT FICA Tax Payable—OASDI   ACCOUNT NO. 232

DATE		ITEM	POST REF.	DEBIT	CREDIT	BALANCE	
						DEBIT	CREDIT

ACCOUNT FICA Tax Payable—HI   ACCOUNT NO. 233

DATE		ITEM	POST REF.	DEBIT	CREDIT	BALANCE	
						DEBIT	CREDIT

ACCOUNT FUTA Tax Payable   ACCOUNT NO. 241

DATE		ITEM	POST REF.	DEBIT	CREDIT	BALANCE	
						DEBIT	CREDIT

ACCOUNT SUTA Tax Payable   ACCOUNT NO. 251

DATE		ITEM	POST REF.	DEBIT	CREDIT	BALANCE	
						DEBIT	CREDIT

PROBLEM 8-7—CONTINUED

ACCOUNT Linda Nickerson, Capital   ACCOUNT NO. 311

DATE	ITEM	POST REF.	DEBIT	CREDIT	BALANCE	
					DEBIT	CREDIT

ACCOUNT Linda Nickerson, Drawing   ACCOUNT NO. 312

DATE	ITEM	POST REF.	DEBIT	CREDIT	BALANCE	
					DEBIT	CREDIT

ACCOUNT Professional Fees—Dentistry   ACCOUNT NO. 411

DATE	ITEM	POST REF.	DEBIT	CREDIT	BALANCE	
					DEBIT	CREDIT

ACCOUNT Professional Fees—Oral Hygiene   ACCOUNT NO. 412

DATE	ITEM	POST REF.	DEBIT	CREDIT	BALANCE	
					DEBIT	CREDIT

PROBLEM 8-7—CONTINUED

ACCOUNT Laboratory Expense   ACCOUNT NO. 511

DATE	ITEM	POST REF.	DEBIT	CREDIT	BALANCE	
					DEBIT	CREDIT

ACCOUNT Laundry Expense   ACCOUNT NO. 512

DATE	ITEM	POST REF.	DEBIT	CREDIT	BALANCE	
					DEBIT	CREDIT

ACCOUNT Payroll Taxes Expense   ACCOUNT NO. 532

DATE	ITEM	POST REF.	DEBIT	CREDIT	BALANCE	
					DEBIT	CREDIT

ACCOUNT Rent Expense   ACCOUNT NO. 541

DATE	ITEM	POST REF.	DEBIT	CREDIT	BALANCE	
					DEBIT	CREDIT

PROBLEM 8-7—CONTINUED

ACCOUNT Salary Expense — ACCOUNT NO. 551

DATE	ITEM	POST REF.	DEBIT	CREDIT	BALANCE	
					DEBIT	CREDIT

ACCOUNT Telephone Expense — ACCOUNT NO. 561

DATE	ITEM	POST REF.	DEBIT	CREDIT	BALANCE	
					DEBIT	CREDIT

ACCOUNT Utilities Expense — ACCOUNT NO. 567

DATE	ITEM	POST REF.	DEBIT	CREDIT	BALANCE	
					DEBIT	CREDIT

ACCOUNT Miscellaneous Expense — ACCOUNT NO. 581

DATE	ITEM	POST REF.	DEBIT	CREDIT	BALANCE	
					DEBIT	CREDIT

PROBLEM 8-7—CONCLUDED

4.

Dr. Linda Nickerson, Dentist

Trial Balance

April 30, 200X

Account Name	Debit	Credit
Cash		
Office Supplies		
Professional Supplies		
Professional Equipment		
Accumulated Depreciation—Professional Equipment		
Office Equipment		
Accumulated Depreciation—Office Equipment		
Employees' Income Tax Payable		
FICA Tax Payable—OASDI		
FICA Tax Payable—HI		
FUTA Tax Payable		
SUTA Tax Payable		
Linda Nickerson, Capital		
Linda Nickerson, Drawing		
Professional Fees—Dentistry		
Professional Fees—Oral Hygiene		
Laboratory Expense		
Payroll Taxes Expense		
Rent Expense		
Salary Expense		
Telephone Expense		
Utilities Expense		
Miscellaneous Expense		

PROBLEM 8-8—CONTINUED
1., 4., 9., AND 10.

General Ledger

ACCOUNT Cash   ACCOUNT NO. 111

DATE	ITEM	POST REF.	DEBIT	CREDIT	BALANCE DEBIT	BALANCE CREDIT

ACCOUNT Medical Supplies   ACCOUNT NO. 114

DATE	ITEM	POST REF.	DEBIT	CREDIT	BALANCE DEBIT	BALANCE CREDIT

ACCOUNT Prepaid Insurance   ACCOUNT NO. 118

DATE	ITEM	POST REF.	DEBIT	CREDIT	BALANCE DEBIT	BALANCE CREDIT

ACCOUNT Medical Equipment   ACCOUNT NO. 161

DATE	ITEM	POST REF.	DEBIT	CREDIT	BALANCE DEBIT	BALANCE CREDIT

PROBLEM 8-8—CONTINUED

ACCOUNT Accumulated Depreciation—Medical Equipment   ACCOUNT NO. 161.1

DATE	ITEM	POST REF.	DEBIT	CREDIT	BALANCE	
					DEBIT	CREDIT

ACCOUNT Office Equipment   ACCOUNT NO. 171

DATE	ITEM	POST REF.	DEBIT	CREDIT	BALANCE	
					DEBIT	CREDIT

ACCOUNT Accumulated Depreciation—Office Equipment   ACCOUNT NO. 171.1

DATE	ITEM	POST REF.	DEBIT	CREDIT	BALANCE	
					DEBIT	CREDIT

ACCOUNT Employees' Income Tax Payable   ACCOUNT NO. 231

DATE	ITEM	POST REF.	DEBIT	CREDIT	BALANCE	
					DEBIT	CREDIT

PROBLEM 8-8—CONTINUED

ACCOUNT FICA Tax Payable—OASDI   ACCOUNT NO. 232

DATE	ITEM	POST REF.	DEBIT	CREDIT	BALANCE	
					DEBIT	CREDIT

ACCOUNT FICA Tax Payable—HI   ACCOUNT NO. 233

DATE	ITEM	POST REF.	DEBIT	CREDIT	BALANCE	
					DEBIT	CREDIT

ACCOUNT Cecil Burt, Capital   ACCOUNT NO. 311

DATE	ITEM	POST REF.	DEBIT	CREDIT	BALANCE	
					DEBIT	CREDIT

ACCOUNT Cecil Burt, Drawing   ACCOUNT NO. 312

DATE	ITEM	POST REF.	DEBIT	CREDIT	BALANCE	
					DEBIT	CREDIT

PROBLEM 8-8—CONTINUED

ACCOUNT Income Summary　　　　　　　　　　　ACCOUNT NO. 331

DATE	ITEM	POST REF.	DEBIT	CREDIT	BALANCE DEBIT	BALANCE CREDIT

ACCOUNT Professional Fees　　　　　　　　　　ACCOUNT NO. 411

DATE	ITEM	POST REF.	DEBIT	CREDIT	BALANCE DEBIT	BALANCE CREDIT

ACCOUNT Laundry Expense　　　　　　　　　　ACCOUNT NO. 512

DATE	ITEM	POST REF.	DEBIT	CREDIT	BALANCE DEBIT	BALANCE CREDIT

PROBLEM 8-8—CONTINUED

ACCOUNT Payroll Taxes Expense

ACCOUNT NO. 532

DATE	ITEM	POST REF.	DEBIT	CREDIT	BALANCE	
					DEBIT	CREDIT

ACCOUNT Rent Expense

ACCOUNT NO. 541

DATE	ITEM	POST REF.	DEBIT	CREDIT	BALANCE	
					DEBIT	CREDIT

ACCOUNT Medical Supplies Expense

ACCOUNT NO. 543

DATE	ITEM	POST REF.	DEBIT	CREDIT	BALANCE	
					DEBIT	CREDIT

ACCOUNT Depreciation Expense—Medical Equipment

ACCOUNT NO. 547

DATE	ITEM	POST REF.	DEBIT	CREDIT	BALANCE	
					DEBIT	CREDIT

PROBLEM 8-8—CONTINUED

ACCOUNT Depreciation Expense—Office Equipment   ACCOUNT NO. 548

DATE	ITEM	POST REF.	DEBIT	CREDIT	BALANCE	
					DEBIT	CREDIT

ACCOUNT Insurance Expense   ACCOUNT NO. 549

DATE	ITEM	POST REF.	DEBIT	CREDIT	BALANCE	
					DEBIT	CREDIT

ACCOUNT Salary Expense   ACCOUNT NO. 551

DATE	ITEM	POST REF.	DEBIT	CREDIT	BALANCE	
					DEBIT	CREDIT

ACCOUNT Telephone Expense   ACCOUNT NO. 561

DATE	ITEM	POST REF.	DEBIT	CREDIT	BALANCE	
					DEBIT	CREDIT

PROBLEM 8-8—CONTINUED

ACCOUNT Legal Expense ACCOUNT NO. 564

DATE	ITEM	POST REF.	DEBIT	CREDIT	BALANCE DEBIT	BALANCE CREDIT

ACCOUNT Utilities Expense ACCOUNT NO. 567

DATE	ITEM	POST REF.	DEBIT	CREDIT	BALANCE DEBIT	BALANCE CREDIT

ACCOUNT Miscellaneous Expense ACCOUNT NO. 581

DATE	ITEM	POST REF.	DEBIT	CREDIT	BALANCE DEBIT	BALANCE CREDIT

PROBLEM 8-8—CONTINUED

2., 3., 9. and 10

CASH RECEIPTS JOURNAL

Page 19

DATE		DESCRIPTION	POST REF.	GENERAL DR.	PROFESSIONAL FEES 411 CR.	CASH 111 DR.

Total debits _____

Total credits _____

CASH PAYMENTS JOURNAL

Page 23

DATE	CHECK NO.	DESCRIPTION	POST REF.	GENERAL DR.	SALARY EXPENSE 551 DR.	EMP. INC. TAX PAY. 231 CR.	FICA TAX PAY. OASDI 232 CR.	FICA TAX PAY. HI 233 CR	CASH 111 CR

Total debits _____

Total credits _____

PROBLEM 8-8—CONTINUED

2. and 9.   **GENERAL JOURNAL**   PAGE 7

	DATE		DESCRIPTION	POST REF.	DEBIT	CREDIT	
1							1
2							2
3							3
4							4
5							5
6							6
7							7
8							8
9							9
10							10
11							11
12							12
13							13
14							14
15							15
16							16
17							17
18							18
19							19
20							20
21							21
22							22
23							23
24							24
25							25
26							26
27							27
28							28
29							29
30							30
31							31
32							32
33							33
34							34
35							35
36							36

PROBLEM 8-8—CONTINUED

2. and 10.   **GENERAL JOURNAL**   PAGE 8

	DATE		DESCRIPTION	POST REF.	DEBIT	CREDIT	
1							1
2							2
3							3
4							4
5							5
6							6
7							7
8							8
9							9
10							10
11							11
12							12
13							13
14							14
15							15
16							16
17							17
18							18
19							19
20							20
21							21
22							22
23							23
24							24
25							25
26							26
27							27
28							28
29							29
30							30
31							31
32							32
33							33
34							34
35							35
36							36

PROBLEM 8-8—CONTINUED

5.—10. (*continued on facing page*)

Dr. Cecil Burt, Physician and Surgeon

Work Sheet

For the Year Ended December 31, 200X

	ACCOUNT TITLE	TRIAL BALANCE DEBIT	TRIAL BALANCE CREDIT	ADJUSTMENTS DEBIT	ADJUSTMENTS CREDIT
1	Cash				
2	Medical Supplies				
3	Prepaid Insurance				
4	Medical Equipment				
5	Accum. Depr.—Medical Equipment				
6	Office Equipment				
7	Accum. Depr.—Office Equipment				
8	Employees' Income Tax Pay.				
9	FICA Tax Payable—OASDI				
10	FICA Tax Payable—HI				
11	Cecil Burt, Capital				
12	Cecil Burt, Drawing				
13	Professional Fees				
14	Laundry Expense				
15	Payroll Taxes Expense				
16	Rent Expense				
17	Medical Supplies Expense				
18	Depr. Exp.—Medical Equip.				
19	Depr. Exp.—Office Equip.				
20	Insurance Expense				
21	Salary Expense				
22	Telephone Expense				
23	Legal Expense				
24	Utilities Expense				
25	Miscellaneous Expense				
26					
27					
28					
29					
30					
31					
32					
33					

PROBLEM 8-8—CONTINUED

5.—10.

Dr. Cecil Burt, Physician and Surgeon

Work Sheet

For the Year Ended December 31, 200X

ADJUSTED TRIAL BALANCE		INCOME STATEMENT		BALANCE SHEET		
DEBIT	CREDIT	DEBIT	CREDIT	DEBIT	CREDIT	
						1
						2
						3
						4
						5
						6
						7
						8
						9
						10
						11
						12
						13
						14
						15
						16
						17
						18
						19
						20
						21
						22
						23
						24
						25
						26
						27
						28
						29
						30
						31
						32
						33

PROBLEM 8-8—CONTINUED

5.

| Dr. Cecil Burt, Physician and Surgeon |
| Trial Balance |
| For the Year Ended December 31, 200X |

PROBLEM 8-8—CONTINUED

8.

Dr. Cecil Burt, Physician and Surgeon

Income Statement

For the Year Ended December 31, 200X

Dr. Cecil Burt, Physician and Surgeon

Statement of Owner's Equity

For the Year Ended December 31, 200X

PROBLEM 8-8—CONTINUED

8.

Dr. Cecil Burt, Physician and Surgeon

Balance Sheet

December 31, 200X

PROBLEM 8-8—CONCLUDED

11.

Dr. Cecil Burt, Physician and Surgeon

Post-Closing Trial Balance

December 31, 200X

Account Name	Debit	Credit
Cash		
Medical Supplies		
Prepaid Insurance		
Medical Equipment		
Accumulated Depreciation—Medical Equipment		
Office Equipment		
Accumulated Depreciation—Office Equipment		
Employees' Income Tax Payable		
FICA Tax Payable—OASDI		
FICA Tax Payable—HI		
Cecil Burt, Capital		

CHALLENGE PROBLEM
1. — 3.

CASH RECEIPTS JOURNAL   Page 5

DATE	DESCRIPTION	POST REF.	GENERAL DR.	OTHER INCOME 421 CR	PROFESSIONAL FEES 411 CR.	CASH 111 DR.

Total debits   _____

Total credits   _____

challenge problem—continued

1. — 3.

CASH PAYMENTS JOURNAL

Page 23

DATE	CHECK NO.	DESCRIPTION	POST REF.	GENERAL DR.	SALARY EXPENSE 551 DR.	EMP. INC. TAX PAY. 231 CR.	FICA TAX PAY. OASDI 232 CR.	FICA TAX PAY. HI 233 CR	CASH 111 CR

Total debits   _____

Total credits   _____

CHALLENGE PROBLEM—CONTINUED
1. and 2.

DAILY SERVICE RECORD FOR

DATE	NAME OF PATIENT AND CODE	DIAGNOSTIC	PREPARATIVE	RECONSTRUCTIVE
	AMOUNTS FORWARDED			

KIND OF

CHALLENGE PROBLEM—CONCLUDED

1. and 2.

THE MONTH OF APRIL 200X

SERVICE			PATIENT ACOUNTS		
RESTORATION	PREVENTATIVE	MISCELLANEOUS	CHARGE	CASH SERVICES	PAYMENTS